Day Hikes in the Columbia River Gorge

Hiking Loops, High Points, and Waterfalls within the Columbia River Gorge National Scenic Area

Don J. Scarmuzzi

WESTWINDS
PRESS®

Library of Congress Cataloging-in-Publication Data

Scarmuzzi, Don.
  Day hikes in the Columbia River Gorge : hiking loops, high points, and waterfalls of the Columbia River Gorge National Scenic Area / Don J. Scarmuzzi.
    pages cm
  Includes index.
  ISBN 978-1-941821-70-1 (paperback)
  ISBN 978-1-941821-90-9 (hardbound)
  ISBN 978-1-941821-89-3 (e-book)
  1. Hiking—Columbia River Gorge (Or. and Wash.)—Guidebooks. 2. Columbia River Gorge National Scenic Area (Or. and Wash.)—Guidebooks. 3. Natural history—Columbia River Gorge National Scenic Area (Or. and Wash.) I. Title.
  GV199.42.C64S36 2015
  796.5109795'4—dc23

                    2015006590

Design by Vicki Knapton
Edited by Mindy Fitch

Cover photo by Don J. Scarmuzzi. A rare angle of the striking Elowah Falls shows one of two cascades directly above the main 213-ft drop visible to most people, to bring the total height to around 289 ft.

WestWinds Press®
An imprint of

GRAPHIC ARTS
BOOKS®
P.O. Box 56118
Portland, OR 97238-6118
(503)254-5591
www.graphicartsbooks.com

Dedicated to Miley Cyrus

who said, "There's no right or

wrong, success or failure."

CONTENTS

OVERVIEW MAP

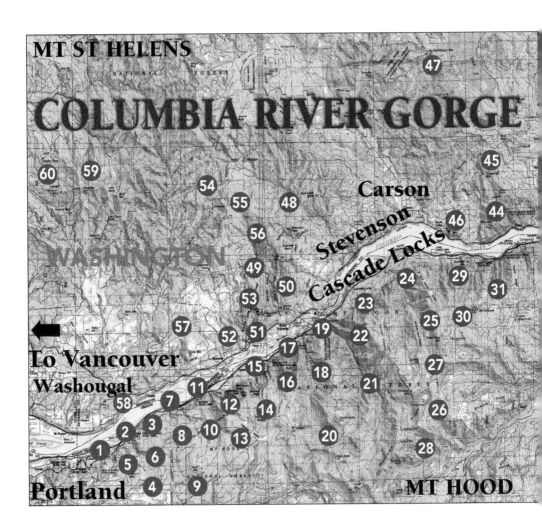

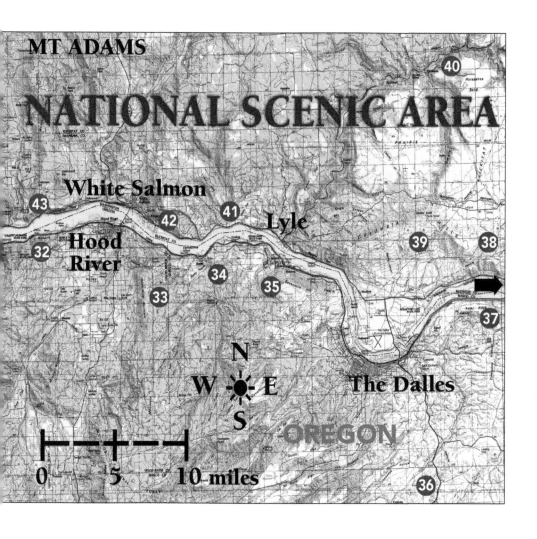

MT ADAMS

NATIONAL SCENIC AREA

40

White Salmon

43

42

41

Lyle

39

38

32

Hood
River

34

35

33

37

N

W ☀ E

S

The Dalles

OREGON

0   5   10 miles

36

PREFACE

Day *Hikes in the Columbia River Gorge* is the most straightforward, colorful, easy-to-follow hiking guide for the region, offering easygoing jaunts, exceptionally steep scrambling, long hikes, and everything in between. Within these pages you'll find a new day hike or a new perspective on an old one. Truthfully, you don't even have to get out of your car to see many of the waterfalls and surprises—but I really hope you will!

The Columbia River Gorge National Scenic Area truly unveils itself as you come at it from the west on I-84 E, within seconds of driving under the bridge at exit 22 for Corbett. And it's just as dramatic when you round the turn to Cape Horn from Washougal in Washington. Traveling 50 million years back in time to the Miocene era, then the Pleistocene era, the Columbia Gorge was formed due to several volcanic eruptions and uplift that produced the Cascades. Then, at the end of the last Ice Age some 15,000 years ago, the Missoula Floods carved the deep walls of columnar basalt, exposing layers of lava.

Anyone who lives in or regularly visits Oregon and Washington should make a pilgrimage to this National Scenic Area several times a year. True, the Gorge can be rather ominous at times during the cold season. But hiking during the best days of fall, winter, and spring can help you stay in shape for the more demanding treks of summer, when the snows melt higher up in the Cascade Mountains and volcanoes of the Pacific Northwest. And no matter the season, the Gorge is boundless with beauty and wildlife. For more about the history of the area, and contemporary conservation efforts, visit:

- www.fs.fed.us/rtr/forests/crg.shtml
- www.summitpost.org/columbia-river-gorge/153977
- en.wikipedia.org/wiki/Columbia_River_Gorge

This guide begins with a counterclockwise tour of the awe-inspiring 85-mi corridor from Troutdale in Oregon all the way to the Deschutes River State Recreation Area past The Dalles. Then we cross the river into Washington, working west through a kaleidoscope of options, climates, and high points by several charming towns over a smaller, picturesque highway to Washougal and Vancouver.

Each hike begins with essential information about elevation, distance, duration, and difficulty level, and trip reports point out any noteworthy and important tidbits. Elevation information includes the highest point (or points) and destination of a hike as well as the maximum vertical gains you will experience along the trail. Difficulty level is broken up into five categories: *easiest* (short hike, little to no elevation change, sometimes paved, ideal for families and novices), *moderate* (more elevation change but easier than most), *strenuous* (longer hike, some steeps, some trail-locating, use of hands for balance), *very challenging* (fairly long hike, sustained steeps for thousands of feet, bushwhacking, GPS helpful, use of hands necessary), and *expert-only* (very long hike, extreme steeps, overgrown paths, exposed cliffs, climbing-type moves possible though no climbing gear necessary, traction devices at times). While the Overview Map on pages 6 and 7 covers the entire region, each hike is covered by maps that detail smaller subsections of the Gorge.

For the sake of brevity, I use the abbreviations TH (Trailhead) and FR (Forest Road). Likewise I refer to the Pacific Crest Trail (also known as the Pacific Crest National Scenic Trail or Crest Trail) as the PCT and the Historic Columbia River Highway as the HCRH. A switchback is a spot in a trail that zigzags sharply, whether once or fifty times. A shoulder is a rise or small ridge. "Exposure" refers to an individual's level of risk of falling where a tumble would be fatal. A trail section described as "airy" is exposed to some degree, with drop-offs. Exercise extreme caution in such areas.

Parking is free at some THs, as with the first hikes described in the Oregon section. Other THs require a daily use fee, which can be covered by a Northwest Forest Pass in Oregon or a Northwest Forest Pass or Discover Pass in Washington. Both passes are good for one day ($5 to $10 per vehicle on average) or one year (about $30 to $35) and are available online, at ranger stations, and at many retail outlets. It's always helpful to look up your hike online for particulars on payment at the TH and to make sure trails are open. At times a trail may be inaccessible due to rock- or landslides, flooding, road closures, fires, snow, or for wildlife protection. Even the most popular trails can be inaccessible for quite a while, as when the hundred-year-old Benson Bridge near Multnomah Falls was struck and severely damaged by a large falling rock in early January 2014, closing easy access to several popular trails until Memorial Day. Similarly, a landslide a mile up Oneonta Trail late in 2014 took out the safest and easiest approaches to Triple Falls (and Upper Oneonta Falls) for several months into 2015. Check the following sites for trail and road conditions, updates on fording occasional creeks, pass information, and the latest trip reports:

- www.fs.usda.gov/activity/crgnsa/recreation/hiking/
  ?recid=29872&actid=50
- gorgefriends.org
- www.portlandhikers.org
- www.wta.org

To be safe, avoid leaving any valuables in your vehicle before getting on the road. And if you feel the need to bring dogs remember the Gorge is not ideal for them considering the terrain, poison oak, ticks, and the likelihood of scaring off any wildlife, but if you must please follow the leash law in all areas for safety and for the courtesy of other hikers.

Of course, remember to be prepared no matter how short or long your day hike will be, especially October through April. Every year Search and Rescue (SAR) saves tourists and locals alike who come ill-equipped for quickly changing weather or get lost on one of many unmarked roads or trails not found on most maps. Keep in mind that the sun sets much earlier during fall and winter than in summer at this longitude. Conditions in the mountains, and specifically in the center of the Gorge, can change rapidly and may contrast drastically from that of Portland or The Dalles.

A dry, warm hiker is a happy hiker! Bring some if not all of the following on your day hike: your experience, a friend, lots of layers (polyester or not) including backup rain gear and dry socks, sunscreen, water or purifier, food, flashlight or headlamp, map or GPS or compass, fresh batteries, smartphone backup battery charger, first aid kit with an emergency blanket, lighters, knife, insect repellent, whistle—and a sense of humor.

OREG

GON

(West to East)

OREGON

ELEVATION: 655 ft, with around 500 ft vertical gain

DISTANCE: 2¼ mi round-trip loop

DURATION: Less than 2 hours round-trip

DIFFICULTY: Easiest. Paved trail for the Lower falls, wide, popular year-round, slightly steeper path for the loop to the Upper falls

TRIP REPORT: Many of the shorter hikes with waterfalls within the Columbia River Gorge can be combined with other nearby falls and cascades to get the most out of your day. This first hike can be joined with the next few or any number of the year-round waterfalls in this illustrious geographical zone. More than a hundred waterfalls appear from January through April or May within the Gorge along the Columbia River, which splits the states of Washington and Oregon in quite a dramatic fashion all the way from Astoria near the Pacific Ocean well past The Dalles at the E end of the Gorge. There is no fee to park, and pit toilets are present.

Classic shot of the impressive Latourell Falls; the very first and closest waterfall to Portland from the Gorge is also one of the easiest to view!

TRAILHEAD: Guy W. Talbot State Park. Drive 30 minutes from downtown Portland on I-84 E to exit 28, stay on E Bridal Veil Road ½ mi, and turn right (W) on the HCRH (US-30) 2¾ mi. If coming from Hood River or the E, take exit 35 (Ainsworth State Park), and continue more than 10 mi W on the HCRH to the signage and small parking off the S side of the road at Guy W. Talbot State Park. Did you notice all the other waterfalls visible in spring months the last mile to Latourell Falls?

ROUTE: Take the paved trail on the right from the parking area past the Latourell Falls sign for the shortest walk (about a hundred yards) down to see the Lower falls, which are a long narrow band with a 224-ft straight drop next to a backdrop of brightly colored rock. For a better look and to see Upper Latourell Falls, take

Always better than expected and double-tiered Upper Latourell Falls.

the paved trail to the left (S) from the parking lot steeply to begin past the first immediate overlook of the falls. Continue up the wide dirt path, keeping the Lower falls in sight until near the top, where you should use utmost caution if you decide to duck the cable opposite the bench, as many others have, and descend the side path briefly to the very top. The rocks and roots are solid but there is no guardrail, so unless you're wearing a parachute, please be extra mindful of your steps near the edge and avoid completely if wet. In more than ½ mi arrive at the bridge crossing below the Upper falls on the maintained trail. You will pass a couple shortcuts across the creek (skipping the Upper falls) over big logs when they are dry, as you ascend more switchbacks and then actually go down a bit to the alcove. This slightly twisting, 2-tiered waterfall plunges 125 ft into a pool surrounded by columnar basalt, which seems to be the general theme of some of the other falls coming up, all with different flows.

Finish the clockwise loop across the bridge and hike down a couple switchbacks and along easily with an alright view of the Columbia River and a poor view of the Lower falls if you go right (E) at the third upcoming fork. The first 2 forks work down across the creek over big logs, the second one with a spur to the little viewpoint and the rest of the trail. Walk left (W) from the third fork on the main trail up a few feet past another somewhat safer viewpoint, then down switchbacks and turns lazily (even heading S and W, seemingly away from the TH for a moment) back to the highway, crossing it wisely. Move down the stairs right of the picnic area on the paved trail ¼ mi, including right around the corner and up painlessly under the Interstate bridge to the base of Latourell Falls. Cross the stream over the footbridge and walk up to your vehicle in a hundred yards. So many waterfalls and walks to go, and so much time!

> **"How we spend our days is, of course, how we spend our lives." —Annie Dillard**

ELEVATION: 180 ft, with 50 ft vertical gain as you walk down to begin and then regain that to finish

DISTANCE: Less than ¼ mi round-trip max

DURATION: 10–20 minutes round-trip

DIFFICULTY: Easiest. Paved but bumpy, extremely brief

TRIP REPORT: Combine these falls with the adjoining hikes on your waterfall tour. This is the shortest hike is this book! No fee or restroom.

TRAILHEAD: From Portland, take I-84 E to exit 28, stay on E Bridal Veil Road ½ mi, turn right (W) on the HCRH 1½ mi to the signed TH on the left, with the trail beginning directly under the sign. Park on either side of the road and follow the trail down, although you can see the falls from the TH and bridge.

ROUTE: Take the stairs from the parking area down to the falls along the stone guardrail on the paved but semi-rough trail. It's difficult to get to a worthy angle of these falls without a pretty rough bushwhack, which is not recommended. A few more drops above and below are officially part of the 220-ft falls, but only the 92-ft, 2-tiered hourglass is visible adjacent from the viewpoint (this portion is also known as Youngs Creek Falls). There is a small double drop straight on from the end of the walkway, which floods at times.

Slice of Shepperd's Dell Falls and the trail flanking under the HCRH bridge, also known as Shepperd's Dell Bridge or Young Creek Bridge.

3 BRIDAL VEIL FALLS

ELEVATION: 145 ft at the main falls; 420 ft at Middle Bridal Veil Falls; 650 ft at the bottom of Upper Bridal Veil Falls; with vertical gains of 115 ft as you descend 75 ft or so, then hike up 40 ft to the Lower falls, 220 ft from the HCRH bridge for the Middle falls, and only 200 ft down, then back up, from NE Palmer Mill Road for the Upper falls

DISTANCE: Only about 1 mi or less round-trip for each of the falls, and it is nearly impossible to connect them as there is only an established trail for Bridal Veil Falls

DURATION: ½–1 hour round-trip for Bridal Veil Falls; 1 hour round-trip bushwhack paths for Middle or Upper falls

DIFFICULTY: Mix of easiest (for Bridal Veil Falls or Overlook Loop Trail, obvious, short, wide) and strenuous (for the other falls, narrow, over-grown, Upper Bridal Veil Falls path very steep)

TRIP REPORT: Bridal Veil Creek contains several commendable falls within a fairly brief distance. Between the Middle and Upper falls alone are a few more significant drops in the stream, and Upper Bridal Veil Falls is secretly among the best in the Gorge! This will become more apparent in the future if the proposed loop trail connecting the Middle and Upper falls is constructed (shown in darker purple on the map, p. 46). Also noteworthy from the main TH is the Overlook Loop Trail to Bridal Veil Falls State Scenic Viewpoint. This 1-hour-round-trip, ½-mi-all-access, interpretive, flat, paved path avoids the local falls and remains on a bluff overseeing the river corridor to the cliff bands at Cape Horn in Washington, which are home to many thin waterfalls during winter and spring. No fee required at any TH. Restroom found only at (lower) Bridal Veil Falls.

TRAILHEAD: Bridal Veil Falls State Park. From Portland, take I-84 E to exit 28, stay on E Bridal Veil Road ½ mi, turn right (W) on the HCRH less than 1 mi to Bridal Veil Viewpoint for the Lower falls and Overlook Trail. Park at the tiny pull-out right and W of the bridge over Bridal Veil Creek on the HCRH (or at the nearby official parking lot and walk along the road) for the Middle falls alone. For the Upper falls, from the paved parking on the right at the bottom, park exactly 1 mi up nearby NE Palmer Mill Road (a few feet after Angel's Rest TH on the left, S) to a tiny pullout on the right 75 ft past a 25-ft cascade and creek that runs under the road through a pipe. Alternatively, if you don't like the few pullout choices for

Intriguing and off the beaten path is Middle Bridal Veil Falls.

the Upper falls along the steeper road, you can park where it's flatter and there is more space ½ mi farther up where it meets NE Brower Road. Palmer Mill Road is a mostly steep and narrow dirt road: watch out for local traffic, occasional rockslides, wildlife, and pedestrians.

ROUTE: For Bridal Veil Falls, walk E from the parking lot past the restroom on a paved (then dirt) path down 2 switchbacks to cross Bridal Veil Creek over a wooden bridge. Hike up briefly and steeply to the official viewing platform of the 2-tiered, 120-ft waterfall. Adventurous types walk out onto the big boulder at the base of the falls for a close-up and to get sprayed on a hot summer day, although these can be reached year-round. Return the same way as an observably super-steep and slippery bushwhack path empties onto the narrow highway above and is not open for safety reasons.

To reach the more attention-grabbing Middle Bridal Veil Falls (about 60 ft high, 20 ft wide), bushwhack from the HCRH bridge and stay W of the creek the entire route as you start past the old gate. Fork left and head down to the water instead of walking too far to the right and onto private property (indicated by many signs). Then follow Bridal Veil Creek up the thin to absent path more than ½ mi to a beautiful angle below the Middle falls. Consider wearing gloves and

Also difficult to access but exemplary is Upper Bridal Veil Falls.

pants, as bushes over your head, prickly vines, water crossings, and a steep hillside adjacent the creek all make these falls tricky to visit. A longer, cascading waterfall without a huge flow is seen across the creek just before Middle Bridal Veil Falls. Return the same way.

For Upper Bridal Veil Falls, walk from 850 ft in elevation on Palmer Mill Road down a small shoulder in front of the pullout/parking area easily for about 75 ft. With nothing more than a bushwhack path, the route should still be discernible as the hillside is too steep for a trail into Bridal Veil Creek everywhere else along Palmer Mill Road. The path in the trees splits into two 8 ft past a narrow moss-covered tree at the base of another fir, one moving extremely steeply to the left (SW) and slightly more in the direction of the Upper falls. The preferred trail that moves to the right past the moss-covered tree before the steeps follows the shoulder almost immediately more in the center and straight down (W) the sometimes slippery and difficult to locate bushwhack path super-steeply. The most solid path moves slightly more right (NNW) after the initial steep descent. You can partially see and hear the falls for most of the short hike. Follow the creek side briefly on the left (E) as far as you wish, with barely any trail to a get closer look, and watch for spray from the nearly 100-ft-tall, almost 50-ft-wide stately falls. Be careful near the creek's slick edge, and return the same way ¼ mi and 20 minutes back up to Palmer Mill Road. Or sign up for more punishment by bushwhacking with no solid trails ¼ mi or more downstream (staying E of the creek) to at least a couple of other sets of falls above Middle Bridal Veil Falls.

ELEVATION: 2149 ft, with 2000 ft vertical gain from the bottom of NE Palmer Mill Road

DISTANCE: 5 mi up, 10 mi round-trip

DURATION: 2 hours up, 3 hours round-trip

DIFFICULTY: Moderate. Steep gravel road walking from bottom into paved and then slightly overgrown trail, not popular, possible bushwhacking, no signs

One of many auto carcasses found scattered mostly on the Oregon side of the Gorge in the strangest of places, and mostly reclaimed by the rain forest.

TRIP REPORT: This little summit is just S of the peaceful Bridal Veil Creek area, which is tucked between a fairly busy zone at the W end of the Gorge. One reason this high point is rarely visited is that there is nothing much to see from the top. The other is that you have to walk up a gravel (then paved) road whether you begin from the bottom or top of NE Palmer Mill Road to get to the old-growth bright green forest on Pepper Mountain (top saves a few miles round-trip). Several paths and old roads surround the double summit block, most of which are quite overgrown and not recommended. No fee or restroom.

TRAILHEAD: From Portland, take I-84 E to exit 28, stay on E Bridal Veil Road ½ mi, turn right (W) on the HCRH a hundred feet, and turn left on NE Palmer Mill Road to park at the small paved area immediately on the right. Or drive rather steeply about 1½ mi up the narrow gravel road to a barricade at the intersection with NE Brower Road. No parking at the actual TH 1½ mi N of Larch Mountain Road.

ROUTE: Walk steeply slightly more than 1½ mi SSE up NE Palmer Mill Road, passing a small cascade that is piped under the road, and continue from the intersection and barricade down right (WSW) on NE Brower Road across the bridge over Bridal Veil Creek. Some of the Columbia River across to the cliffs and possible waterfalls of Cape Horn can be seen through the trees from Palmer Mill Road and above. Climb the rough, narrow gravel road more than ½ mi as it turns to pavement without sidewalks on a switchback for 2 mi more to the trail on the left (E). Pass by "shooting prohibited" signs along the road that should make you feel safe and possibly a fenced-in dog that will bark at you en route.

Western poison oak is rampant throughout the region, this one with leaves young and glistening with toxic oil. "Leaves of three, run away!" Or something like that . . .

The main trail will be at about 1600 ft in elevation and less than ¼ mi past where E Haines Road intersects from the right to meet NE Brower Road. There is a narrow, open wooden shed across the gravel road from a yellow mailbox. This brief segment resembles someone's driveway, but the trail breaks away from FR-1500 and the private property in ¼ mi. Continue up right from the residence on the thin, lively road without any difficulty ¼ mi to a juncture, staying right (S) a hundred yards to a small saddle between summits. Leave the wider old road to bushwhack the overgrown path to the left. This begins the final stretch winding to the flat top, a small grassy opening surrounded by a few tiny pines. Glimpses of Larch Mountain and Mount Hood can be seen ESE through the woods near the summit meadow, and Silver Star Mountain can barely be made out to the N. Return down the same way, being careful along less-traveled Brower Road to Palmer Mill Road. If you parked at the Palmer Mill Road and Brower Road intersection, you could extend your day by hiking up to Devil's Rest and return to the same locale (*see* hike 6).

5 | ANGEL'S REST LOOP

ELEVATION: 1500 ft at the bench on the tip of Angel's Rest; 2120 ft at the Foxglove Trail–Devil's Rest intersection for a loop without Devil's Rest; with vertical gains of 1350 ft, and almost 2000 ft for the loop

DISTANCE: 2¼ mi up, 5-plus mi round-trip with side trails; 7¾ mi round-trip loop without Devil's Rest; 11 mi round-trip long loop including Devil's Rest and Wahkeena Creek

DURATION: 1 hour to Angel's Rest, 2–3 hours round-trip; 3½–5 hours round-trip loops

DIFFICULTY: Mix of moderate (steady, wide, very popular, steep drop-offs at times) and strenuous for loops (ups and downs, narrow trails above Angel's Rest, overgrown)

Sunset over the Columbia River from Angel's Rest.

TRIP REPORT: Angel's Rest and Devil's Rest are vastly different: the former leads to a wide-open, dreamy overlook of the Columbia River Gorge with dramatic cliffs on 3 sides, while the latter leads to an uneventful little rock- and moss-covered high point in the thick emerald woods with no views outward. (That said, Devil's Rest is included in hike 6 because of the pleasurable loops that pass near it and the superior overlook ¼ mi NE of the summit.) Look for a less-traveled clockwise loop from this TH to Angel's Rest, then Devil's Rest, and down Bridal Veil Creek on Palmer Mill Road back to your car. Or try it counterclockwise. The shorter loop above Angel's Rest is described below. Also note that "Angels Rest" and "Devils Rest" are accepted spellings, as the USGS is slowly phasing out apostrophes on its maps.

At only 30 minutes from Portland, Angel's Rest is among the busiest trails in the Gorge, and for good reason. It is lovely when it's sunny and warm and is a great spot for watching sunsets. However, it can also be bitterly cold in winter and windy enough to make safety on the bluff a genuine concern. Remember that being in the Gorge means dressing appropriately and wearing reliable hiking shoes. Be mindful of younglings, pets, and yourself near the cliffs at the top, as falls have proven to be fatal. During drought years or slower starts to winter, Angel's Rest to Devil's Rest might remain snow-free until February or so and stay fairly busy. No fee or restroom.

TRAILHEAD: From Portland, take I-84 E to exit 28, stay on E Bridal Veil Road ½ mi, and turn right (W) on the HCRH, where the Angel's Rest TH resides immediately on the right. When that lot fills, park on the side of the HCRH, or better yet at the bottom of nearby NE Palmer Mill Road opposite the highway (which has its own access trail). Coming from Hood River or the E, take exit 35 (Ainsworth State Park) from I-84 and continue W on the HCRH 7 mi to the TH on the right.

ROUTE: Cross the old highway carefully from Angel's Rest TH, or begin from Palmer Mill Road TH on Angel's Rest Trail 415: both trails meet in a couple hundred yards, where you work through the fern-lined forest and rocky trail more than ½ mi to partially obscured looks of Coopey Falls. Be attentive while leaning over the cliffy area for the best picture. Unfortunately the optimal place to see the 150-plus-ft, horseshoe-type falls is from private property below, although a future loop trail may pass by there. Continue a few feet to Upper Coopey Falls, where 30–35 ft of cascading water can be seen somewhat from the main trail or the short spurs, with the second path being better. The third look is from directly on top of the drop. Again, be careful.

Cross the footbridge over the creek and waterfall area at ¾ mi from the TH, and hike more steeply through about 17 switchbacks as the terrain changes and you ascend an old burn area. The vistas to the Gorge open up and the trail crosses a scree field as it switches back one more time to a junction at the top. Turn left (N) and be careful on the thin ridge section for Angel's Rest, or head to the right (S) for the loops above. Even if Angel's Rest isn't your goal it's still a worthwhile pit stop. Scramble immediately up the boulders in the center of the ridge without difficultly, then continue more easily over the large bluff. A bench located at the end for the curious can be attained by working around the rock on the right, then contouring 50 ft left (W) on the paths through some tight brush.

Because of a few distinct air masses affecting weather in the region and the mountains in the Gorge rising more than 4000 ft from the Columbia River, the area is known for extremely windy days. It can go from a refreshing breeze on a hot summer day to relentless, freezing, lashing gales in winter. On a clear day see

Looking down from Upper Coopey Falls.

Portland, Silver Star Mountain, Beacon Rock, and the tops of Mount St. Helens and Mount Adams in Washington, and up and down the Columbia River unobstructed. You should be able to find your own piece of the rock somewhere on the bluff unless it's a summer weekend.

Return easily back down to the TH or continue on 1 of at least 3 loops. Once you are beyond Angel's Rest on the trail in the woods arrive at the first intersection above 2 switchbacks. The longer 6½-mi loop (above Angel's Rest) past Wahkeena Spring is not a favorite because it misses most of the falls in that area and has steeper ups and downs. But have at it: exercise is exercise! For that you take the left above Angel's Rest on Trail 415, and traverse E (then descend NE) for 2 mi to the Wahkeena Spring junction, where you stay right (E) on Trail 420 for ½ mi up to Devil's Rest Trail 420C on the right. Follow the narrow path S up steeper switchbacks 1½ mi as the views unfold along the ridge, especially at one sweet overlook onto a short spur trail right (N 100 ft) ¼ mi below Devil's Rest. Follow the main trail more steeply, then more easily, past the moss-covered boulders and woods near Devil's Rest (spur path 50 ft right to the summit), and continue less than 2 mi (NW) down the ridge to Angel's Rest.

The shorter 3¼-mi loop (from Angel's Rest) travels left or straight from the low intersection above Angel's Rest. If you turn left (E, clockwise) on Angel's Rest Trail 415, contour along the cliff band more than a mile to a nice camp by the creek, then soon to the right-hand turn onto Foxglove Trail. Walk S up with a pleasant grade ½ mi on the main path to the end, where a turn to the left (SE) will take you steeply up to Devil's Rest in ½ mi and a turn to the right (NW) will take you back down the little ridge to Angel's Rest on Foxglove Trail/Way (future continuation of Devil's Rest Trail 420C).

If you take the shorter loop counterclockwise above Angel's Rest, continue on Foxglove Way (Devil's Rest Trail) straight up the hill and ridge SE easily for ½ mi through the thicker forest, where an optional, slightly overgrown side trail to the left (Foxglove Way) heads more narrowly (NE) and more quickly to Foxglove Trail closer to Angel's Rest Trail 415 (*see* the maps, pps. 31, 46, 47, 48). Stay on the main path to the right instead up to 2 more junctures. The first in ½ mi is an obscure path option that turns to the right (S) for ¼ mi, then left (E) for a mile toward Devil's Rest narrowly but fairly interestingly without being too steep. Follow the small sign on the tree that leads you left instead on the main path through the bog, as you descend a bit more than ¼ mi to the continuation of the signed Foxglove Trail on the left, with the right-hand fork leading steeply to Devil's Rest in almost ½ mi. Continue left (N) for the shorter loop minus Devil's Rest and walk down the wide path with ease around ½ mi to Trail 415. Turn left (W) for 1½ mi on a relaxed traverse to Angel's Rest, passing a small camp with a hidden waterfall just below it to begin. Descend 2 switchbacks above Angel's Rest, and then it's about 2½ mi more to the TH.

6 DEVIL'S REST LOOP

ELEVATION: 2408 ft, with 2300-plus-ft vertical gain from all THs

DISTANCE: 4¼ mi up from Angel's Rest TH, 8½ mi round-trip; 10½ mi round-trip loop with Bridal Veil Creek from Angel's Rest TH; 3¾ mi from Wahkeena TH, 7½ mi round-trip; almost 5 mi from Multnomah Falls TH, 9½ mi round-trip loop with Wahkeena Falls Trail, ending almost ¾ mi from Multnomah Falls TH

DURATION: 2 hours up, 3 hours round-trip from Angel's Rest TH; 4 or more hours round-trip for most loops

DIFFICULTY: Strenuous for all routes. Solid, well marked, wide trails, semi-disorientating near the top, brief steeps

TRIP REPORT: Spring and early summer (for wildflowers) and winter seem to be the best seasons to visit this area. It's a bit overgrown above Angel's Rest in late summer around Foxglove Way/Trail, but the snowshoeing in deep winter around the top and upper Bridal Veil Creek is delightful. A GPS device is helpful but not necessary. No fee. Year-round restrooms only at Multnomah Falls TH.

TRAILHEAD: There are at least 3. Use Angel's Rest TH or park at the bottom of nearby NE Palmer Mill Road for the closest and most straightforward routes or for a long loop with Bridal Veil Creek. From Portland, take I-84 E to exit 28, stay on E Bridal Veil Road ½ mi, and turn right (W) on the HCRH where Angel's Rest TH resides on the right. When that lot fills, park at the bottom of nearby NE Palmer Mill Road opposite the HCRH. If Devil's Rest is your only goal, you can also cheat by driving around 1½ mi (steeply for most in 2WD) up the narrow but smooth dirt road to the barricade, walking up Bridal Veil Creek and the road/trail from there. For the waterfall route from Wahkeena TH, take I-84 E to exit 28, and continue left (E) up at the intersection on the historic highway (US-30) for 2½ mi to the TH on the right. From the E, take exit 35 (Ainsworth State Park) and continue W 4½ mi on the HCRH to the TH on the left. For Multnomah Falls TH, take I-84 to exit 31 and find parking in the center of the Interstate.

ROUTE: For the most popular route, *see* hike 5 and scamper up to Angel's Rest, turning right near the top of the bluff to continue up 2 switchbacks in the trees. Hike straight up the little ridge for about 1¼ mi to a fourth juncture. The second one ½ mi past the left on Trail 415 is the rest of the more faded Foxglove Way path that moves left (NE; see the old sign on the tree left of the path) and meets Foxglove Trail just before Trail 415. Hike to the right instead through the bright green forest without any difficulty ½ mi to the third confluence, and see the sign on the tree pointing left (E) to stay on the main trail.

The lush forest on Foxglove Way/Trail.

The more overgrown side path to the right (S) is less traveled but also heads toward Devil's Rest and could be used as another little loop option around the summit. For this simply turn right for ¼ mi and then turn sharply to the left (E) on the next semi-obscured path for about a mile. You must leave this path before the denser woods to bushwhack left (NNW) with no trail a hundred yards over to Devil's Rest Trail, which soon passes within 50 ft of the actual summit. Or as most people would do from the third juncture and side path loop option, stay left on the main trail more than ¼ mi as you walk down a bit through the bog to the Foxglove Trail (fourth) juncture. Avoid this left (N) for now and continue almost ½ mi more steeply up to Devil's Rest, following the signage. Near the apex, leave the main trail to walk the spur path left (N) 50 ft over to the moss-covered boulders and rocks that comprise the high point in the thick forest. No use lingering or following an ultra-steep bushwhack path N of the summit toward the Gorge.

From the overlook near Devil's Rest to the Gorge and Mount Adams.

Return down Foxglove Trail/Way or take one of the loop variations (*see* the map, p. 31). The foremost one takes you back the same way to Foxglove Trail less than ½ mi W of Devil's Rest and then down the widening trail to the right (N) easily ½ mi to Angel's Rest Trail 415, where you turn left (W) and traverse effortlessly more than a mile to Foxglove Way. Turn right narrowly and soon down the pair of switchbacks to Angel's Rest, where you walk left (W) after a thin section above the bluff to finish 2¼ mi down to the TH.

A noteworthy clockwise loop from the summit is to drop into Bridal Veil Creek by taking Palmer Mill Road down to your vehicle near Angel's Rest TH. For this loop, continue NNE from the summit on Devil's Rest Trail down more steeply ¼ mi to a clear side trail (left 100 ft) and superior overlook near a huge boulder attached to a cliffy area. See the Gorge, Silver Star Mountain, and three big Cascaders in Mount St. Helens, Mount Rainier (barely), and Mount Adams. Proceed NE when you are ready for almost ¾ mi along the cliff line in the trees, crossing a couple of bridges while descending, then arrive at a very short path to the right at a "trail" sign. Move right (E) for 75 ft as Devil's Rest Trail heads N down the ridge, and then turn right again (S) on FR-129 (broad) for almost ½ mi, passing a wide saddle (2200 ft) halfway to Bridal Veil Creek.

Turn right (SW) past the big brown steel gate onto the old road (FR-1520, NE Palmer Mill Road), which has a steady grade and is easy to follow along the year-round gorgeous stream. Hike 3 mi, taking the last fork to the right to the nearby barricade, then more than 1½ mi steeply down the gravel road to Angel's Rest TH. Bridal Veil Creek is wonderful and has been one of the best-kept secrets in the Gorge until recent years. Hike and snowshoe this loop in winter when snow covers the higher portions of the trails, or travel counterclockwise from Palmer Mill Road to the saddle, Devil's Rest, Angel's Rest, and down.

For the counterclockwise loop or route from the bottom of NE Palmer Mill Road, walk more steeply at times up the gravel road, stepping aside for light local traffic. About ¼ mi past the little cascading waterfall that travels under the road through a wide pipe, it begins to level out somewhat to the junction with NE Brower Road. Walk 3 mi more past the barricade straight up the old road/trail to the turnoff, as Bridal Veil Creek is audible the entire way. A small mountain has been robbed of its forest to the right (S) through the trees, but hang in there. The route makes up for it directly above, when the trail meets the stream again and is quite charming up to the intersection with FR-129 to Devil's Rest.

Turn left (N) on FR-129 (small sign and a large brown steel gate to the right of the road) from the top of Bridal Veil Creek, less than ¼ mi up to a wide saddle at 2200 ft, just SSE of Devil's Rest. For a less desirable bushwhack, head left at the nearby fork on the saddle, continuing W onto FR-150 (no sign); even though there may be a few branches and logs strewn across the start at a little makeshift camp, no signs indicate any closures. From this path, stay left at a foggy upcoming fork where the path becomes more solid again for another ½ mi easily through the woods. The wider section narrows for a bit and begins to descend toward Angel's Rest. When the forest thins again somewhat, bushwhack right (N) off trail about a hundred yards to the Devil's Rest Trail, where you turn right to the summit.

For the preferred but slightly longer route on solid trails, walk straight from the saddle at about 2200 ft less than ¼ mi, turn left (W) at the next nondescript junction for only 75 ft, then left again (SW) onto Devil's Rest Trail 420C. Take it almost ¾ mi up without trouble to a spur path on the right (N 100 ft) to a terrific vista of the Gorge. Finish ¼ mi more steeply SSW through the thicker woods to the summit area. Return the same way or *see* above for many loop options to the same TH.

From Wahkeena TH, walk to the right (W) up the stone stairs or over the footbridge and steadily up Trail 420, with only 1 switchback to the base of Wahkeena Falls, then more steeply up a dozen paved switchbacks before the spur to Lemmon's Viewpoint is obvious to the right. Continue up the rise to the left (S) on the dirt trail and through 6 steep switchbacks past the fanned-out Fairy Falls beside the trail. Above the falls and 5 more switchbacks you can fork left (NE) or right (S), as both trails meet above. Note, however, that going left on the more narrow Vista Point Trail 419 may be more attractive. It's about ¼ mi longer up a little shoulder but has less pesky switchbacks; just ignore an overgrown side path steeply down N to mostly obscured vistas en route. Turn left (E) when Trail 419 ends at the juncture with Trail 420 for 50 ft, then veer right (S) onto Devil's Rest Trail 420C.

Hike up steeper switchbacks on Trail 420C more than 1½ mi to the top, discovering views out to the Gorge, especially at the short spur path to the right (N 100 ft) ¼ mi from Devil's Rest. A loop around the summit can be accomplished if you continue down Devil's Rest Trail less than ½ mi W from the top to the ½-mi-long easy Foxglove Trail on the right (N). Then turn right on Angel's Rest Trail 415 around a mile down and over to Wahkeena Springs and onto Wahkeena TH (N, left) down steeply on Trail 420, or Multnomah Falls TH (E, straight/right) also on Wahkeena Trail 420 to Trail 441 and down.

Typical scene from Bridal Veil Creek in summer.

From Multnomah Falls TH and viewing area, follow the paved and popular Trail 441 a mile up over the Benson Bridge to the top of the falls and many paved switchbacks. Walk more easily down over the bridge, crossing the creek, and continue steadily up the ancient, waterfall-lined canyon another mile. Turn right on Wahkeena Trail 420 from Trail 441 as it traverses up almost a mile steadily to Devil's Rest Trail 420C on the left. Follow it up switchbacks steeply to begin as above, then walk more easily with decent views unfolding before the denser woods at Devil's Rest.

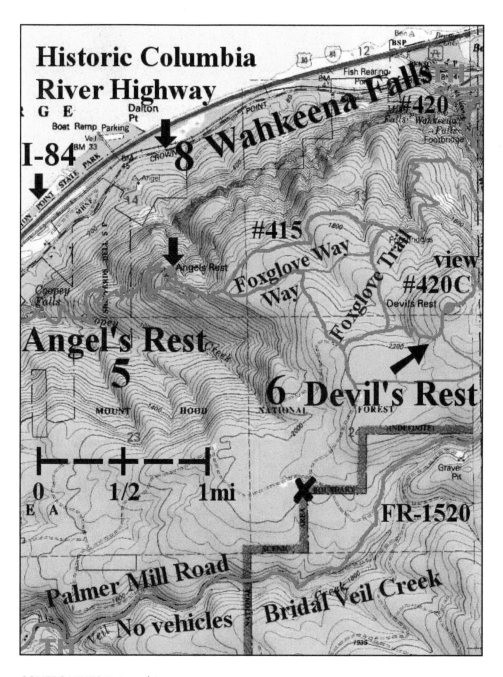

COVERS HIKES 5, 6, and 8

ELEVATION: 825 ft, with about 900 ft vertical gain

DISTANCE: 1¼ mi up to the Upper Viewpoint above the falls, 2½ mi round-trip

DURATION: 1 hour up, 2–3 hours round-trip with breaks

DIFFICULTY: Moderate. Paved switchbacks, steady, fairly steep grade, relatively brief, most popular

Windy fall day at Multnomah Falls with the 100-year old Benson Bridge between drops.

TRIP REPORT: Spring and early summer are best for maximum flow; deep winter with snow is fun too, but the trail freezes at times around the Multnomah Falls Foot (Benson) Bridge over the creek. As with seasonal Mist Falls and nearby Shady Creek Falls to the W, at least a couple of extra ribbons stream down to the right of Multnomah Falls at times, and all are visible from the Interstate parking lot. Multnomah Falls has the tallest drop in the state at 542 ft, with a 69-ft lower tier, and another 10 ft above the top of the biggest drop for around 630 ft total. In spite of the more than 2 million annual visitors, it's still worth checking out the attention-grabbing falls several times a year to get the full flavor. You can always add a loop hike or use this TH to get to several magnificent points higher up.

Try to carpool if possible: a gate at the main entrance coming from Portland on I-84 E automatically closes access to the parking lot at capacity on busy days and weekends in the summer. If you find the gate closed, do not wait there under any circumstances (both dangerous and illegal) but drive to exit 35 (Ainsworth), turn right 4 mi W on the HCRH to the alternative parking closer to Multnomah Falls Lodge (multnomahfallslodge.com), or visit other local waterfalls until parking in the main lot becomes available. No fee. Restrooms with flush toilets present.

TRAILHEAD: Multnomah Falls Lodge. Drive 35 minutes from Portland or Hood River on I-84 to exit 31 for Multnomah Falls in the center of the Interstate. Or take exit 28 (Bridal Veil) from the W and continue left (E) on the HCRH 3 mi to more parking closer to the lodge.

ROUTE: From the main huge parking lot, walk under the Interstate through the little tunnel—as millions of people have before you—over to the day lodge with a restaurant, gift shop, more parking, and a coffee and snack stand, and head left a few feet over to the first official viewing area. Break out your waterproof camera (or protect the one you've got from spray) as you start up the paved path, Larch Mountain Trail 441, from the viewpoint below the 69-ft tier. After the switchbacks and more angles of waterfalls, cross the Benson Bridge high above Multnomah Creek directly over the lowest tier. From there you will have a superior look at one of the most distinguished waterfalls around for hundreds of miles. You can really feel the roar of the falls in the vertical amphitheater!

Oregon's highest waterfall at the edge of the lush, temperate rain forest.

Continue above the bridge to the first switchback sign on a little shoulder; it's not really a switchback, but it's still a way to count and remind yourself you have a ways to go. Hike up 3 true switchbacks in the woods before Gorge Trail 400 moves left (E) on the third switchback. Climb the paved trail another ½ mi to the top, where you will be glad to have thought ahead to bring water. Descend briefly and turn right on the designated unpaved trail less than ¼ mi down the switchbacks and easy grade to the Upper Viewpoint and platform at the top of Multnomah Falls. Here you can check out the uppermost 10-ft tier before the water dives unknowingly off the edge of the cliff for the plunge of a lifetime. Just make sure you don't do the same! (Having said that, it would be nice if the platform extended a few more feet so that you could actually see the water plummeting down. But I can understand why they didn't do that for a couple of good reasons.) While checking out the Gorge, notice all the little people at the bottom and how small your car looks. Return the same way.

ELEVATION: 600 ft at Lemmon's Viewpoint; 1600 ft at the high point on Trail 420; with vertical gains of 550 ft and 1550 ft

DISTANCE: 1½ mi round-trip short walk; almost 6 mi round-trip loop with Multnomah Falls

DURATION: Around 1 hour round-trip for Lemmon's Viewpoint, 2½–3½ hours round-trip loop

DIFFICULTY: Mix of moderate (wide, steep, paved switchbacks, brief) and strenuous (loop with some steeps, good signage, rocky at times, drop-offs near several waterfalls)

Favorite ingrown Gorge trail sign!

TRIP REPORT: Winter and spring months are best, when local waterfalls are raging and other routes higher up are still covered by snow. However, the Multnomah Creek area freezes at times on Larch Mountain Trail 441 during winter, making passage difficult without traction devices. Also occasional rock-, mud-, and snowslides throughout the waterfall area along Multnomah Creek can make travel impossible, so be sure to check for any trail closures before getting on the road, especially in winter. Wildflowers abound during warmer months, May through July. Wahkeena TH is also a sizeable day-use area with several picnic tables spread out. No fee at either TH. Restrooms open only in summer or year-round at Multnomah Falls Lodge.

TRAILHEAD: Hike the loop in either direction from 2 THs within ½ mi of each other. Take exit 31 from I-84 coming from Portland or Hood River to start at Multnomah Falls main TH. Some prefer the quieter Wahkeena TH from exit 28 (Bridal Veil), continuing left (E) on the HCRH 2½ mi. From the E, take exit 35 (Ainsworth State Park) and continue 4½ mi W on the historic highway (US-30) to Wahkeena TH.

A hiker crosses the bridge at Wahkeena Falls.

ROUTE: Wahkeena Falls can be seen from the TH—a long, twisting, triple-cascading waterfall coming down elegantly 242 ft. For a better look at the falls, cross the little footbridge to the right or take the stone stairs right of the creek and footbridge to the big trail sign, and amble easily to another bridge you can see above only ¼ mi and 1 switchback away. If you start at Wahkeena TH and hike the loop counterclockwise, you get to finish with the granddaddy Multnomah Falls after passing more than 8 waterfalls on the loop!

To hike the loop clockwise from Wahkeena Falls, however, begin from the smaller Wahkeena TH up the paved ramp (wheelchair accessible to an immediate viewpoint), then steps, and walk left (E) immediately almost ½ mi on Return Trail 442 to the W end of the parking strip by the old highway less than ¼ mi from Multnomah Falls Lodge. This will be the return route on a counterclockwise loop if you began from the lodge. *See* hike 7 and trudge to the top of Multnomah Falls on the paved trail as it turns to dirt crossing Multnomah Creek over the bridge at 1¼ mi from that TH. Continue up the steep, Jurassic-like canyon on the right (W) side of the creek, passing 35-ft Dutchman Falls and others, then the attractive taller, narrower Weisendanger Falls at 50 ft high. Not much higher is the photogenic 55-ft-high Ecola Falls, whose top you

Pristine Weisendanger Falls in early winter.

walk right by on the narrow rocky trail. After almost a mile from the bridge crossing the stream above Multnomah Falls on Trail 441, leave that trail to turn right (W) on Wahkeena Trail 420.

Your waterfall tour isn't quite complete yet. Traverse the forest much more easily up less than a mile to the next junctures. Skip Devil's Rest Trail on the left, and debate turning right in 50 ft on Vista Point Trail 419 (slightly longer at less than a mile but down a nicely graded shoulder) or staying on Trail 420 less than ½ mi to the next intersection. At the intersection, the left fork heads toward Angel's Rest past Wahkeena Spring, while turning right (N) keeps you on the Wahkeena Trail, heading steeply down many switchbacks 1½ mi as the path becomes paved and leads to Wahkeena TH. Both Trail 419 and Trail 420 meet above Fairy Falls. *See* the end of hike 6 and below for a more detailed description.

For the counterclockwise loop from Wahkeena TH, begin right (W) after a few stone stairs or over the footbridge, and walk ¼ mi up 1 long switchback to the stone bridge crossing the middle of Wahkeena Falls. Continue past the bench ½ mi more steeply up 12 paved switchbacks with a decent grade to a flatter junction. Turn right 50 ft for Lemmon's Viewpoint at an overlook with a chained guardrail and expansive views of the Gorge and Benson Lake below. If the family's not all tuckered out, resume the loop—it's just starting to get good!

So you like switchbacks? Since the alternative is to hike straight up and down a mountain, switchbacks can be much-appreciated allies. Walk steeply less than ½ mi up the rocky trail, crossing the creek 2 times over bridges, then climb 6 switchbacks to Fairy Falls, a pretty small (20 ft high) but charming, fanned-out cascade just off the trail. Directly above the falls and 5 more switchbacks is the junction with Vista Point Trail 419 to the left and the wider Wahkeena Trail 420 on a switchback to the right. Both meet in about a mile, with the main trail being a bit shorter and having more switchbacks. Both are nice.

If you went right up 3 more switchbacks, turn left (E) at the next juncture to stay on Trail 420 and begin the traverse up almost ½ mi, then down less than a mile to the end at Multnomah Creek.

Follow the remarkable canyon a mile down left on Larch Mountain Trail 441 past a handful of dazzling waterfalls (*see* above), then check out Multnomah Falls from the platform at the top of the falls or save it for another day. Descend the final mile over steeply paved switchbacks on the suddenly busy trail. Cross the Benson Bridge below Multnomah Falls and walk down to finish. Stay left (W) at the lodge to the end of the parking area to find the short and scenic Return Trail 442 if you parked at Wahkeena TH.

9   LARCH MOUNTAIN LOOP

ELEVATION: 4055 ft on Sherrard Point, with vertical gains of 200 ft from the large parking area near the top, 1400 ft from a big curve on Larch Mountain Road where many people park for a short hike or loop (1800 ft gain), and 4035 ft from Multnomah Falls TH (4400-plus ft from Wahkeena TH)

DISTANCE: ¼ mi from the picnic area above the main parking lot, ½ mi round-trip; 1¾ mi up, 3½ mi round-trip with no loop from the NW ridge and a big curve on Larch Mountain Road; 6½–7 mi round-trip loop around the crater and extinct volcano from a big curve on Larch Mountain Road or from the top and large parking area; 8 mi up the NW ridge directly (11 mi up through the crater to the E ridge), 16–20 mi round-trip loop from Multnomah Falls TH in the Gorge (8½ mi up from Wahkeena TH, 11½ mi climbing up through the crater to the E ridge for the longest routes)

DURATION: 10–15 minutes up, 1 hour max round-trip; 1 hour up from a big curve on Larch Mountain Road, 2½–3 hours round-trip with no loop and with a break; 4 hours round-trip loop around the crater of Larch Mountain; 7–10 hours round-trip long loop from Multnomah Falls TH (*see* under "Trailhead" for bike loop option)

DIFFICULTY: Mix of easiest (from Larch Mountain parking lot, paved path with stairs near the end, congested in summer), moderate (shorter loop or not, steady, wide, semi-rough path within crater), and very challenging (from Multnomah Falls or Wahkeena THs in the Gorge, steep, very long, decent signage, snow in winter buries route)

TRIP REPORT: Stimulating year-round. Snowshoe and cross-country ski up the closed road and area trails around the top and crater in winter, keeping in mind that it can be windy or foggy on the summit. The road to Larch Mountain is closed past milepost 10 (actually 9½ mi at a big orange gate) from late November through May or June depending on snow coverage. Check for possible road and trail closures online. Sherrard Point is a separate name given to the higher of two points on the summit block of the Larch Mountain shield volcano. The jagged rocky peak itself on Sherrard Point is off-limits outside a high fence surrounding the viewing area. A Northwest Forest Pass or fee are only required to park at the top, where there is a vault toilet.

TRAILHEAD: From Portland, take I-84 E to exit 22, drive steeply 1¼ mi up toward Corbett, turn left (E) on the HCRH (US-30) less than 2 mi, and veer right 10¾ mi (milepost 11½) on Larch Mountain Road to a big curve in the road, where you will park next to (but not blocking) the brown gate on the short side road that is the lower TH after the guardrail. Continue 3 mi more up the road to the end for Sherrard Point alone or for jaunts from the top of Larch Mountain. Take exit 31 from I-84 to Multnomah Falls TH for the long route from the Gorge. And on one more note, you could shuttle a bike to the top of Larch Mountain first, drive down to the HCRH, turn right to Multnomah Falls (passing Crown Point Vista House, Latourell Falls, and others), hike steeply from Multnomah Falls or Wahkeena THs, and then do that bike ride later down the same roads more than 20 mi for a different kind of loop. For a more difficult shortcut, you could also ride down Larch Mountain Road to milepost 4½, take a sharp right on SE Brower Road 3½ mi where it turns into a rather rough and steep gravel road more than ½ mi to the end, turn left (N) around 1½ mi steeply down SE Palmer Mill Road (also gravel) to the HCRH, turn right (E), and ride 3 mi to Multnomah Falls TH.

On a clear day several big Cascade Volcanoes can be seen from Sherrard Point.

ROUTE: Hike a loop in either direction around the crater from the top and highest parking closest to the summit. For the summit alone, from the large parking lot, simply walk about ¼ mi up the coarsely paved Sherrard Point Trail 443 right of the stairs that lead past the picnic area where all paths meet and head more to the right (N) along the high ridge. Take the many steps up to Sherrard Point's fenced-in, sizeable viewing deck to see 5 big Cascade Mountains (plus perhaps Three Sisters and Broken Top more than 100 mi away), the Columbia River, Portland, and Vancouver.

A local's (or cheapskate's) favorite loop is to begin at the quiet lower TH beside a big curve on Larch Mountain Road. This way you are able to finish hiking down to your vehicle instead of up to it (clockwise). For this loop, walk up the closed old rocky road from the big curve and guardrail for ¼ mi and turn left (E) at the juncture down Larch Mountain Trail 441. The trail on the right near the beginning is where you will end the clockwise loop on Trail 441, as you climb up through the crater first and then finish down the NW ridge through the woods easily to your car. After moving more than ¼ mi down the narrow trail, turn right (ENE) at the next intersection more than ¼ mi downhill on Multnomah Creek Way Trail 444. Cross Multnomah Creek over the log bridge and turn right (S) at the immediate juncture to follow the creek upstream, as opposed to hiking steeply NE up to Franklin Ridge Trail 427 on Trail 446.

Travel 3 mi to Oneonta Trail 424 through a marshy area, then a handsome old-growth forest within the crater, with occasional glimpses of the summit over the uneven, rocky, tree-root-covered path before the final slog up to the E ridge and end of the trail. The last mile of the footpath provides much better walking over a kinder grade on the traverse to Trail 424. Proceed right (SW) at the end onto the wider Oneonta Trail, which gently ascends the delightful old forest over the E ridge a mile to a corner on Larch Mountain Road. Simply follow the paved road up more than ¼ mi to the parking lot, then about 100 ft to the paved Sherrard Point Trail right of the restroom and path to the picnic area. Head ¼ mi to the popular viewpoint ascending several stairs to finish. Hang out as long as you wish. As you come down, fork right at any choices, including over the bump that is technically the top of Larch Mountain, and pass an older picnic area along the NW ridge. This is almost as gratifying as the other ridge, with a pleasantly steady grade that takes you almost 1½ mi N to the old road intersection. At the intersection, turn sharply left (NW) ¼ mi to the lower TH on the corner of Larch Mountain Road.

From Multnomah Falls TH, *see* hikes 7 and 8 and continue up Multnomah Creek on Larch Mountain Trail 441 past many decent waterfalls on the left, including Ecola Falls, and then Wahkeena Trail 420 heading right (at 2¼ mi, or 2¾ mi from Wahkeena TH). Stay on the creek and Trail 441 more than a mile. You will pass many little cascades, including one crossing the trail to another signed juncture, this one for Multnomah Basin, where you stay right more than ¼ mi. Skip the

Mount Hood comes out to play from the Larch Mountain viewpoint.

trail for Franklin Ridge on the left (N), saving it for a possible counterclockwise loop option coming down.

Cross 2 more bridges up ¾ mi along the steep creek before you begin to leave it somewhat. Pass by a clearing through a sizeable scree field and then by very big firs on the gravel trail to the next confluence. At 5¾ mi from Multnomah Falls TH, you arrive at a junction with Multnomah Creek Way Trail 444 on the left (E), which turns down briefly and crosses the creek, then either heads right up to Larch Mountain through the crater, or moves left on Trail 446 over to Franklin Ridge or Oneonta Gorge. Stay right (W, then S) instead to skip these options for the most direct route on Larch Mountain Trail, hiking 2 mi more as you steadily climb the NW ridge and turn left (N) onto the paved trail and little ridge for ¼ mi, passing the top of Larch Mountain en route to the summit of Sherrard Point. Spend some quality time at the fenced-in viewing area, which includes several benches and stone-carved inscriptions identifying the big volcanoes.

Hike the NW ridge back down for the most expeditious route on Larch Mountain Trail to Multnomah Falls TH. You can also hike a smaller counterclockwise loop around the crater to Trail 441 (*see* the map, p. 48). Or return down the NW ridge and turn right on Multnomah Creek Way for a Franklin Ridge loop. For this loop, head left (NE) from Multnomah Creek Way immediately once over the log bridge and creek, and climb more steeply to Franklin Ridge Trail (with a separate small creek ford). The latter loop may be preferred if there is too much snow on the E ridge in winter, as the NW ridge is more popular and usually packed out.For the counterclockwise loop to Franklin Ridge from the large parking lot on top of Larch Mountain, however, hike down the E ridge from the main trail on the highest corner of Larch Mountain Road for about 1½ mi, then stay left (W) at the

Bell Creek Trail junction for another mile on Trail 424 to Franklin Ridge Trail 427. Trails converge once again as Trail 446 (coming from Trail 444) meets from the left (W), and about ½ mi farther N is Oneonta Trail 424 heading up over the ridge crest momentarily, then down more steeply (NE) into Oneonta Gorge. This is a hint for another loop hike, as you can take Gorge Trail 400 near the bottom of Trail 424 to Multnomah Falls TH (or Oneonta TH) for a lower 13-mi loop without Larch Mountain but with Franklin Ridge. *See* Triple Falls (hike 12) for that loop, beginning at the Oneonta TH 2 mi E of Multnomah Falls Lodge.

Wander 1½ mi NNW down Franklin Ridge near its end at an obvious sharp switchback to the left (old sign tied together points left). Turn down the main trail SSW easily ½ mi to the end at Larch Mountain Trail, where you turn right (N) 4 mi to Multnomah Falls TH, passing many distinguished waterfalls along the way. A slightly longer option is to continue following Franklin Ridge NW for ½ mi down the narrower path and very last switchbacks on the ridge that end near Nesika Lodge. As soon as you can see the lodge and bunkhouses, stay to the right down to the corner of the wide trail, but turn right for a moment away from the buildings on the thin path 75 ft to Bickel Point, which overlooks the eastern Gorge and Waespe Point. The trails turning left (W) from Franklin Ridge Trail just above the lodge or just left (W) past the lodge itself move SW on a few mellow trails/odd old roads in Multnomah Basin that all travel about a mile down to Multnomah Creek and Trail 441, where you turn right (W, then NW) more than 3½ mi steeply to the TH. *See* the maps on pps. 47, 48 and study hike 10 for this general area, but it's not too tough.

Sunset from the woods near Multnomah Falls before the monsters come out!

ELEVATION: 1880 ft on the trail above Cougar Rock (1733 ft), with 1860 ft or so vertical gain plus 100 ft coming back up from Cougar Rock

DISTANCE: 3 mi up to Bickel Point, 7½ mi round-trip loop with Multnomah Basin

DURATION: 1½ hours for the first 2 mi including up Elevator Shaft, 1 hour more to Bickel Point including the spur to Cougar Rock, 4–5 hours round-trip clockwise loop with Multnomah Basin

DIFFICULTY: Strenuous. Steep rocky switchbacks, scrambling, lack of signage, unusual, narrow ridge to Cougar Rock, some exposure, semi-confusing trails

TRIP REPORT: Best visited April through January, but be aware that snow and ice at the top of Elevator Shaft makes travel tougher in winter. Hiking gloves and pants might prove helpful in this terrain, which includes poison oak. Not a perfect hike for dogs or young children. The preferred route travels clockwise from the suitably named Elevator Shaft to an exciting bouldering option on the short, moss-covered, jagged ridge to Cougar Rock with captivating views. Then you will walk past the occasionally rented-out Nesika Lodge (by the Trails Club of Oregon) to Bickel Point with eastern Columbia River Gorge views. Continue the loop down the mellow, huge Douglas fir–covered plateau in Multnomah Basin, and end more steeply down Multnomah Creek with its many picturesque waterfalls.

Nesika Lodge and Bickel Point are on private property that will remain open to the public as long as people are respectful: as always, pack it out if you have any trash. No fee to park. Restrooms are at Multnomah Falls Lodge, and you can grab a coffee or small snack from the stand.

Friends questioning my hike choice on the long loop from Oneonta Gorge over Franklin's Ridge and down Elevator Shaft!

TRAILHEAD: Multnomah Falls Lodge. Drive 35 minutes from Portland or Hood River on I-84 to exit 31 (Multnomah Falls) leading to a large parking lot in the center of the Interstate.

From Cougar Rock to Little Cougar Rock and the mighty Columbia River.

ROUTE: Walk under the Interstate bridge from the enormous parking lot. Melding in with the camera-happy tourists taking pictures of Oregon's highest waterfall, follow the paved trail up over the Benson Bridge high above Multnomah Creek and proceed by the falls. Continue on the trail up 2 solid switchbacks, ignoring the incorrectly numbered switchbacks, and at the third one (½ mi from TH) stay left (E) on the clearly marked Gorge Trail 400 as you leave the paved trail. Traverse more easily E through the trees ½ mi to a clearing with a huge, steep, moss-covered scree field appearing on your right (S). Stay on the main path until the far side (E) of the scree field, where a faint rocky path heading back W marks the beginning of what turns into almost 50 tight switchbacks to the top of Elevator Shaft! You will rise over 1000 ft in a little more than ½ mi through the thin trees and mossy talus. The rocks are semi-loose and not optimal for hiking, so stay near on the path and enjoy the workout to the top. You end up on the right (W) side and must steeply scramble the last 100 (or so) vertical ft without much of a trail to the middle of the top of the scree field at the trees near a small red flag. Take a breather, check out the sights, including Archer Mountain directly across the Gorge, and continue slightly right (SW) into the trees on the more solid path more easily about 200 ft up to a shoulder of the main ridge.

Climb left (SE) ¼ mi up the super-steep hill and wider ridge, with very few turns and much underbrush. The route finally levels out to where the trail becomes more faint. At about 1700 ft, stay more to the right for a couple minutes, angling away from the cliff band to a vague unsigned intersection. The fork to the right (S) toward Multnomah Basin is the cutoff trail to shorten the loop to the other trails that head S to Multnomah Creek without visiting Cougar Rock or Bickel Point. Stay left (E) instead ½ mi along the cliffy forested easy section by the high point of the trail, then immediately to the junction where the little ridge and faded trail on the left (N) extend almost ¼ mi out to Cougar Rock.

Cougar Rock is not for people afraid of heights. You must be comfortable with bouldering a fairly narrow ridge to a slightly airy summit with some exposure and possible gusting high winds. For this jaunt, hike NNE down about 100 ft in elevation as the path becomes more obvious, first crossing the ridgeline to the right (E), then directly up the steep, moss-covered rocks on the ridge proper to the nearby apex. Cougar Rock is a large, vertical, mostly tree-covered pillar as seen from the Interstate, Multnomah Falls, and Benson State Park below. On the very top is a little boulder with only enough room for one person at a time if you wish. Be cautious around the summit area, as you see the technical climb in Little Cougar Rock and the Interstate just below you to the N with Silver Star Mountain NW and Mount Adams mostly hiding behind Table Mountain across the Gorge to the NE.

Make your way back up to the main trail and turn left (NE) ¼ mi easily down to Nesika Lodge. As soon as you see the lodge, another trail switches back sharply to the right (S), and that is the return trail on the loop through Multnomah Basin, but first walk out to the panorama at Bickel Point. Continue along the road/trail a couple hundred feet as you pass the lodge and red bunkhouses, and move left down the thin access path up at the curve in the old road. Bickel Point has a

Trail marker on a beautiful shortcut in Multnomah Basin.

nice bench and stone wall with a green chain fence, and observes the eastern Gorge and Waespe Point (1112 ft) directly below.

Backtrack to the return trail for the loop, and fork left after the lodge as you walk past the gate. A trail immediately on the left with an old sign leads to nearby Franklin Ridge. From Bickel Point you can also take the old road straight up briefly and continue past Franklin Ridge Trail (forks left) to the same junction above where you turn left (S) on the main trail for ½ mi. Gigantic, old-growth Douglas firs are well over 200 ft in places in Multnomah Basin. Follow a faint and narrow path right for a slightly shorter, more interesting option as the wider road turns left (S, *see* the maps, pps. 47, 48), and immediately notice all the festive holiday bulbs dangling from branches that seem to multiply every year. In only a few minutes the wider road comes back to meet the decorated "Peace and Joy Trail," where you can turn right (W) ¼ mi, then left (S) ¼ mi for the primary route, or you can continue straight (SW) on a rougher trail to the same general vicinity near Multnomah Creek where there are even more trails to confuse you. No worries. Continue SW and S on any one of them, as they all head easily down to the nearby creek and Trail 441 within a few switchbacks.

Turn right (W, then NW more than 3½ mi to the TH) and head more steeply down Multnomah Creek on Larch Mountain Trail 441 past several quality waterfalls, including a long cascading one coming up that overlaps the trail in front of you in splendid fashion. No problem crossing it as you make your way down to the bridge over the creek above Multnomah Falls and to the paved trail. Take it up briefly, then down the final mile and along many switchbacks with the multitudes visiting the state's highest waterfall, who have no idea what a day you've had. They will ask how much farther "it" is, and you will look at them perplexedly but happily and say, "Where are you going exactly?" (Or my standard fallback: "It's around the next corner, not far at all!") Cross the Benson Bridge above the lower falls and head down past Multnomah Falls Lodge to the parking areas.

> **"May your trails be crooked, winding, lonesome, dangerous, leading to the most amazing view."**
>
> **—EDWARD ABBEY**

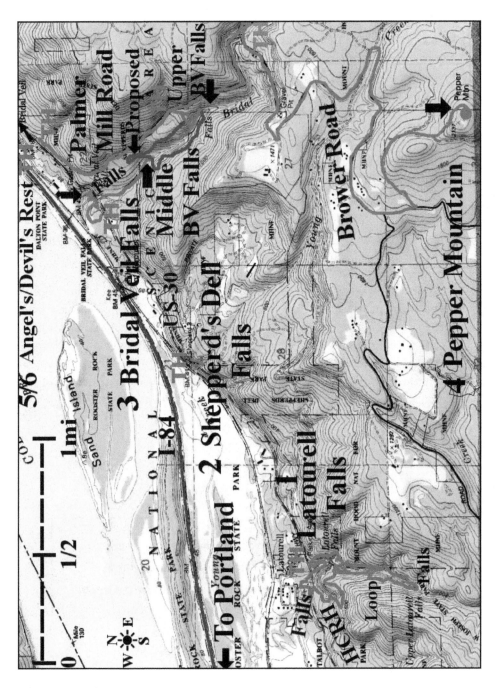

COVERS HIKES 1-6

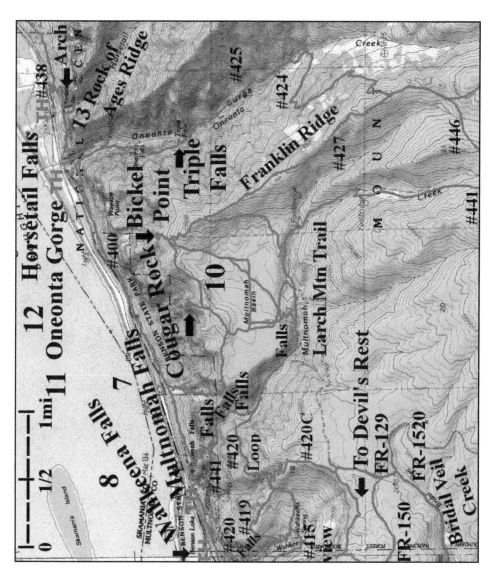

COVERS HIKES 6-13

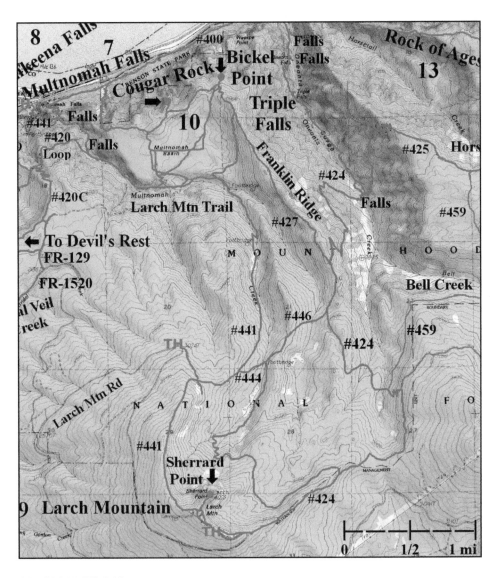

COVERS HIKES 6-13

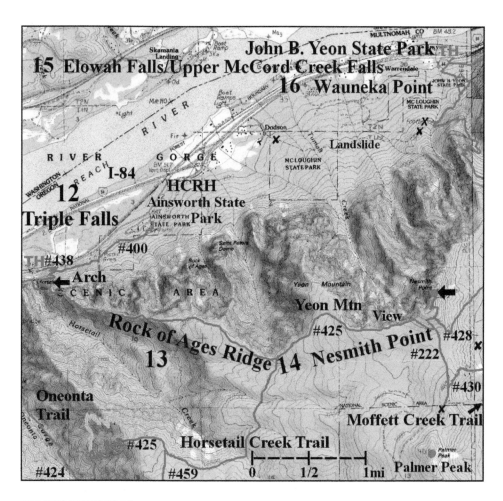

COVERS HIKES 12-14

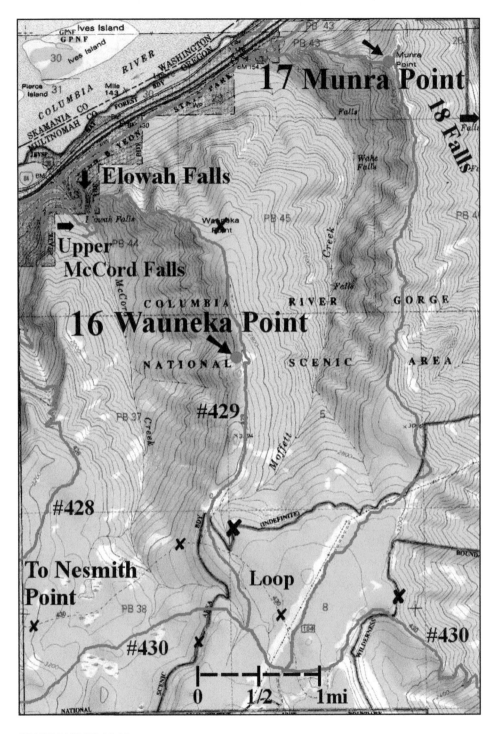

COVERS HIKES 15-18

ELEVATION: 150 ft, with 100 ft max vertical gain

DISTANCE: ½ mi one way, 1 mi round-trip

DURATION: ¾ hour one way, 1½–2 hours round-trip

DIFFICULTY: Moderate. Knee- to chest-deep mandatory creek walking (most likely the latter), potentially slippery large logjam crossing

---

TRIP REPORT: Pick a warm day in May or June for higher flow on Oneonta Falls (also called Lower Oneonta Falls), or wait until late summer through September when the water is warmer and flow has diminished enough so that you won't have to swim for it. Count on getting wet nonetheless and wear appropriate swimwear and decent water shoes with traction for the logjam. Natural dangers and a lack of political will keep this striking slot gorge within a much larger gorge from being very family friendly, although all but the youngest and most elderly seem to attempt it—it's usually teeming with activity on hot days, logjam or not. No fee or restroom, but in summer flush toilets are open ½ mi E of Horsetail Falls TH off the HCRH and also at nearby Ainsworth State Park Campground.

Old stone stairs to Oneonta Gorge from the trailhead adjacent to the mossy rock wall.

TRAILHEAD: From Portland, take I-84 E to exit 28, stay on E Bridal Veil Road ½ mi, continue left (E) on the HCRH 5 mi, just past the Oneonta Trail sign on the right and before the Oneonta Gorge sign to the parking spaces on the right (N), or park after the pedestrian tunnel on the right. Alternatively, take exit 35 (Dodson/Ainsworth) from I-84, turn right (W) on the HCRH 1½ mi, then ½ mi farther past Horsetail Falls. Park on the left before the tunnel and Oneonta Gorge or just after, or at the nearby Oneonta Trail. Only 30 minutes driving from Portland.

ROUTE: The main trail starts down the solid old staircase W of the bridge over Oneonta Creek behind the big sign for Oneonta Gorge. Immediately the tall canyon cliffs begin to close in on you. See the sections of bright yellow lichen attached to rock above to the right. A possible mini-loop to the logjam or alternate path is on the opposite side of the creek E of the bridge to begin or finish, and this is

(Lower) Oneonta Falls and pool at the end of the slender slot gorge.

actually the side of the creek you begin up the logjam if you wish to not get wet right away. Either way, walk a hundred yards to the mouth of Oneonta Gorge, where you must carefully navigate the big boulders and massive logjam. It's tougher when damp or with wet feet (which you will have at some point), so amble slowly and be mindful here and for the rest of the short hike. Also watch for flash floods and falling rock, especially near the base of the falls, even though others will most assuredly be swimming in the pool oblivious to potential danger.

The going is improved past the logjam but deepest at the narrowest point just as soon as you can barely see part of the falls. You could settle for the tease peek if you don't want to commit to the impending bath. Wade through either side of the slender section for about 30 ft or so, keeping in mind that the right (W) side has sloping black rock under the water that might cause you to slip. With low water some can hug the rock wall on the right without getting very wet. Make your way up the creek briefly to the numerous rock piles (cairns) at the end and the 100-ft-high mostly hidden gem. Return the same way when you're ready, back through the chilly water (not as painful now that you're used to it) and carefully over the logjam to the TH on either side of the creek.

ELEVATION: 600 ft at the Triple Falls overlook; 2850 ft on a long loop with Franklin Ridge to Multnomah Falls TH or Oneonta TH; with vertical gains of 550-plus ft for Triple Falls, and about 3000 ft total for the long loop

DISTANCE: 5 mi round-trip lower loop with Ponytail Falls; 13 mi round-trip with side trips on a long loop

DURATION: 2 hours or so round-trip lower loop with Ponytail Falls; 5–6 hours round-trip long loop

DIFFICULTY: Mix of moderate (for lower loop or direct route to Triple Falls, obvious, wide, steeper at times, drop-offs) and strenuous (for upper loops, steadily steep, very lengthy, mostly signed)

TRIP REPORT: Oneonta Gorge is popular with families year-round, although March through June is best for high flow on all the local falls. As trails in the Gorge are notorious for being awfully steep, this one seems quite tame comparatively; still, it gives one a nice sense of accomplishment, with many options for less than a half-dozen miles round-trip. And for those who wish to be challenged, look no further than this scintillating loop ending down Multnomah Basin or Elevator Shaft to the same TH (using Gorge Trail at the bottom) or nearby Multnomah Falls TH (almost 2 mi apart) where you can leave a shuttle vehicle or bike. No fee or restroom, but in summer flush toilets are open ½ mi E of Horsetail Falls TH and at nearby Ainsworth State Park Campground.

Triple Falls is always entertaining as a goal for a shorter family outing with ample excercise.

TRAILHEAD: Take exit 35 (Dodson/Ainsworth) from I-84 in the Columbia River Gorge, turn right (W) 2 mi, just past Horsetail Falls and Oneonta Gorge to Oneonta Trail 424 (with parking spaces opposite the trail on the N side of the

From behind Ponytail Falls on the lively trail.

road) for a preferred counterclockwise lower loop, direct route to Triple Falls, or the long loops up to Franklin Ridge or Rock of Ages Ridge.

ROUTE: Feel free to also begin at Horsetail Falls TH as many others do for the lower loop. For this take a mental picture of the narrow 176-ft Horsetail Falls as it cascades into a pretty pool and head to the left up 5 switchbacks to lovelier Pony-tail Falls (Upper Horsetail Falls). Come around the last corner to see the falls and actually walk behind the 88-ft drop (and 35-ft cascade directly above) to continue up to Triple Falls for the lower loop. You also have the option of taking a rougher but worthwhile side trip ¼ mi to the very top of Ponytail Falls by starting off on the Rock of Ages Ridge Trail if it's not too wet (not ideal for young children). That ultra-steep trail begins left (E) of the falls and left of a tree with exposed roots up the path 150 ft, then right onto the first thin path between a couple of big trees and down to the waterfall. You will have a really cool look straight down the long cascade before it plummets into the pool beneath. Back on Horsetail Falls Trail 438, finish up less than a mile to Oneonta Trail 424 and see below for more detail on the rest of the loops.

For the preferred loop or direct route to Triple Falls, begin the hike W of the short tunnel next to Oneonta Gorge up Oneonta Trail 424 for ¼ mi easily and turn left (E) at the first switchback and shared portion with Gorge Trail 400. Contour up past a pleasant seasonal waterfall streaming down the steep, mossy cliff band to a short-lived mini-loop and side trail option on the left through the trees to views of Archer Mountain across the Columbia River and Beacon Rock farther to the E, with Hamilton Mountain directly behind the monolith. From the main trail, walk briefly past the left (E) turn down to the creek and return loop past Ponytail Falls (½ mi from the first switchback at Trail 400) to hike straight up more steeply less than a mile on the W side of Oneonta Creek to Triple Falls.

Almost ¼ mi up S from the intersection with Horsetail Falls Trail is a steep and mostly obscure path to Upper Oneonta Falls (also called Oneonta Falls, somewhat incorrectly). If you are hiking up, the route drops down to the left off the main trail a couple hundred feet and about ¼ mi on what was once a surprisingly solid traverse path to the base of the rarely visited Upper Oneonta Falls. Only the hardiest of hikers should attempt this bushwhack, as a substantial slide (about 100 ft wide and more than 300 ft long) took out most of the path and part of Oneonta Trail in 2014. Then further landslides late in 2014 occurred in the exact same locale, closing the trail and easy access to Triple Falls for months; the path on the main trail has been stabilized as of April 2015. For Upper Oneonta Falls from the beginning of the slide area, walk left at the fork (steeper right is Oneonta Trail 424) 40 ft and turn left onto the faint path at a narrow, moss-covered tree. A few feet farther the wider old trail forks again, both paths ending at steeper bushwhacks up to the main trail. Move 50 ft down the steep traverse SE on the narrow trail as it becomes super-steep following left of a large downed tree a few more feet. This area will change based on traffic, trail work, and further slides; look for cairns along the bushwhack route and be mindful of falling rocks being inadvertently kicked down from hikers above. Cross over the fat log almost immediately 10 ft to another log crossing. Traverse 10 ft more wisely and begin to descend the steepest part of the rocky gully within the slide area 30 ft or so (just right of a previously cut tree), hanging on to tree roots for assistance. Contour 30 ft across, then climb up briefly to the more solid older path. Ascend the little shoulder easier over an old blowdown and work down to the nearby creek at a makeshift campsite. It's a wonder these falls haven't made it into the mainstream, especially since you can see the top of the waterfall and hear it clearly from the trail above near a few footbridges. A 55-ft lunging drop follows a 10-ft cascade from a moss-lined basalt cliff and amphitheater. Some folks work to the right over the slippery rock, even ducking behind the handsome falls. Return back up carefully when you've had your fill.

For Triple Falls and above, climb right from the first fork at the start of the slide area and traverse the thin rocky route briefly over to more solid ground. Finish up 2 switchbacks on Oneonta Trail to 1 of 2 side paths a few feet, down to the obser-

Inspiring Upper Oneonta Falls worthy of the effort to visit.

vation bench across from Triple Falls (64 ft high). This is an ideal spot for a picnic, but watch for drop-offs: there are very steep ledges most places here and throughout the slender Oneonta Gorge. Hiking off trail directly above the falls near that big log is not safe, as it's usually fairly slippery; one wrong move would be your last.

If you began on Oneonta Trail, turn right for the lower loop onto Horsetail Falls Trail once you are back down to the main intersection, and head down 2 switchbacks immediately to the bridge over the creek. There you will see the mostly unexciting Middle Oneonta Falls at 25 ft high. Downstream from the bridge is the very top of the more interesting but well-hidden Oneonta Falls. Climb 6 quick switchbacks (about 100 ft up) before traversing almost ½ mi N. The top of Oneonta Falls can be seen in winter with no leaves on the trees from a few spots on this trail. Resume down a bit to a short overlook spur trail on the left (N) that continues onto the main path after a great shot of the Gorge and two huge rock columns in Saint Peter's Dome and Rock of Ages to the E. Another ½ mi and you sneak up to Ponytail Falls around the corner (E, then S), as you hear the falls first, then see the water leaping from the steep green cliff band above the clearing into a stunning pool. Walk under the falls and overhang around the alcove and saunter ½ mi down the trail and final 5 switchbacks without much steepness to the Horsetail Falls TH. You have tall, moss-covered basalt cliffs to walk by similar to the W side of the loop near the bottom. Walk left easily ½ mi along the highway and paved trail through the tunnel by the mouth of Oneonta Gorge and to the little parking lot on the right for Oneonta TH.

Keep hiking up 1¼ mi from the bridge directly above Triple Falls (long cascade on the right after the bridge) for a loop with Franklin Ridge to the W or Rock of Ages Ridge to the E of Oneonta Gorge to the same TH. Either way the trek will be much steeper. *See* hike 13 for the latter from the last footbridge crossing to the W side of Oneonta Creek, where you would skip the bridge to stay on the E side of the creek briefly and quite nicely on an amusing alternate trail while avoiding a ford (not the car—the creek, you silly! although I can see arguments for both).

For Franklin Ridge, cross the final bridge in the emerald forest and hike up ¼ mi to the camp and trail on the left. Even if not crossing the water here, take the brief spur (Trail 425) to check out the creek one more time or not, then begin up the steeper trail (Trail 424) and 8 switchbacks 2½ mi SSW to its climax on the forested ridge proper. Curve over the ridge and even descend a bit to the signage, where you turn right (NW) to begin your walk down the delightfully graded Franklin Ridge. After 1½ mi of fairly viewless walking (except for a shot of Mount St. Helens and Mount Adams), take the first switchback left (SSW) near the end of the ridge at an old tied-up sign for ½ mi down to Larch Mountain Trail 441 and Multnomah Creek, where you turn right 4 mi to near the bottom of Multnomah Falls after many more excellent waterfall sightings. Arrange a car or bike shuttle from Multnomah Falls TH or turn right off the paved trail and final switchbacks onto Gorge Trail 400 for 1¾ mi on the traverse undulating E to Trail 424, even dipping down to the old highway once, then finally left at the signed fork ¼ mi to your vehicle at Oneonta TH.

13   ROCK OF AGES RIDGE LOOP

ELEVATION: 800 ft at Rock of Ages Arch; 1300 ft at Devil's Backbone; 3015 ft on the forested basin at the end of the trail; 3301 ft on Yeon Mountain; 3872 ft on Nesmith Point; with vertical gains of 750 ft to the arch, 1250 ft to Devil's Backbone, 3820 ft counterclockwise loop to Nesmith Point, and 3000-plus-ft clockwise loop into Oneonta Gorge to the same general TH area

DISTANCE: ¾ mi up, 1½-plus-mi round-trip for the arch alone; 1½ mi up, 3-plus-mi round-trip for the arch and Devil's Backbone; 13 mi counter-clockwise loop with Nesmith Point down to John B. Yeon State Park (arrange shuttle vehicle or bicycle); 11 mi clockwise loop with Oneonta Gorge

DURATION: ½ hour up, more than 1 hour round-trip; at least 1 hour up to a treeless, rocky protrusion and possible picnic spot on Devil's Backbone, 2–3 hours round-trip; 5–7 hours round-trip long loop with Nesmith Point or Oneonta Gorge

DIFFICULTY: Mix of strenuous (for the arch or Devil's Backbone, route-finding, exceptionally steep, narrow, drop-offs) and very challenging (for loops, few people, Rock of Ages Ridge has more sustained steeps than most known trails in the Gorge, overgrown, narrow, decent signage)

Rock of Ages Arch.

TRIP REPORT: Not recommended in the rain or when muddy. More people may be enticed by the easy creek crossings and multiple waterfalls along the titillating clockwise loop into Oneonta Gorge, than by the tougher loop (or not) with Nesmith Point. Rock of Ages Arch to Devil's Backbone is one of the shortest, most strenuous hikes in the Gorge. It also just happens to include waterfalls, an amusing double arch, cliffs, and superb viewpoints! No fee or restroom, but in summer flush toilets are open ½ mi E of Horsetail Falls TH and at nearby Ainsworth State Park Campground.

TRAILHEAD: Drive 40 minutes from Portland on I-84 E to exit 35 (Dodson/ Ainsworth), and turn right (W) 1½ mi on the HCRH to the Horsetail Falls TH. Parking will be on the right.

ROUTE: Start on Horsetail Falls Trail 438 to the left of the falls up 5 switchbacks and gain elevation quickly ½ mi from the TH. Then work W more into the alcove belonging to Ponytail Falls (Upper Horsetail Falls). As soon as you can see the falls, look to the left (E) for the start of the path to Rock of Ages Arch/Ridge. It lies very steeply left of that big tree with large exposed roots to climb over. Quickly you realize you are undeniably on some sort of trail, although it seems better suited for a herd of Nubian ibex than humans! Here you get a true taste of the challenging and seriously steep hikes that comprise many of the upcoming treks in the Gorge. Even working to Rock of Ages Arch will test your legs and lungs for about ½ mi up the super-steep but solid trail. Poison oak is widespread here for a bit.

A short side path about 150 ft up heads right between a couple of big trees down to the top of Ponytail Falls for an arousing perspective. Climb 100 ft higher and see the trees open somewhat to the left (E) as you can make out the actual ridge. The first path left is more difficult and traverses down, then back up (right), very steeply at a fork to the Rock of Ages Arch. Wait a couple minutes longer for a better trail as soon as you can make out the rocky arch on the ridgeline, and traverse briefly left, then climb a few feet to the arch. Be careful around the cliffy areas near or on top of the arch itself. You'll have a rare angle of the E Gorge and the huge rock pillars of Saint Peter's Dome and Rock of Ages (closer) through the arch itself!

Grind up the ultra-steep path slightly W of the ridge crest until the final hundred yards to even better views from Devil's Backbone less than a mile away. After burning some serious calories, you arrive at the little treeless area and rock overlook to the right that sticks out just far enough to give you fantastic vistas. Horsetail Creek and Oneonta Gorge are W with Franklin Ridge to Waespe Point above, and the Columbia River Gorge is of course well below you. Mount Adams is mostly concealed behind Hamilton Mountain.

Follow the ridge up another hour (more than 1½ mi) SE to the end at Horsetail Creek Trail 425. It's less steep and obvious up the narrow ridge section, with ferns, Oregon grape, and medium-sized pines surrounding you. Then the pitch varies, and becomes quite steep again, before mellowing (thankfully) to the top of the widening ridge. See Mount Adams through the trees and Mount St. Helens near the top. At nearly 1000 ft per mile, Rock of Ages Ridge is still the

Fog layer slowly burns off the river from Devil's Backbone.

local's choice for a full workout while avoiding the hordes on Nesmith Point Trail and others.

Turn right (SSW) on Horsetail Creek Trail unless you are traveling another 900 ft up to Nesmith Point. For that summit, turn left on Trail 425 as the path follows the ridge up NE with a pleasurable grade; you will pass Yeon Mountain (3301 ft), which is barely discernible through the trees to the left (E) and is simply an extension of the main ridge up to Nesmith Point. Soon you will have the best panorama all day (and far superior to that of Nesmith Point) of Mount St. Helens, Mount Rainier, and Mount Adams in one magnificent eyeshot, with the mighty Columbia River 3500 ft below. If you stay on the main path to the end of Horsetail Creek Trail, follow the signage by turning left (N) on Nesmith Point Road 222 as it winds up less than ½ mi to Nesmith Point (passing Nesmith Point Trail 428 on the right, SE). It's 3–4 hours to Nesmith Point from the Horsetail Falls TH, with some views but not 360 degrees. *See* hike 14 to finish the counterclockwise loop to

One of many great perspectives on Oneonta Creek.

Nesmith Point TH, and plan for a shuttle vehicle or bicycle, as Gorge Trail 400 near the bottom is unusable (*see* "Trip Report," hike 19).

Bearing right at the Horsetail Creek Trail sign from the top of Rock of Ages Ridge Trail to Oneonta Creek (4 mi) will take you on a stress-free traverse down the hillside through the thicker forest, crossing 3 little arms of Horsetail Creek easily. After the third stream, at 1 mi from the Rock of Ages Ridge juncture, begin up steadily and sadly (as you hoped you would be finished going uphill for the day) for ½ mi. As soon as you begin to descend, pass the quiet and undervalued Bell Creek Trail 459, which turns left (S) toward Larch Mountain directly, or an even longer loop (15–16 mi) with Franklin Ridge, where you could head W down to Multnomah Creek or E to Oneonta Creek. *See* the maps (pps. 47-49) for help with these options: USGS maps are off somewhat in this general area.

Follow Trail 425 for ½ mi without any difficulty before the ridge thins and begin a series of 15 steady switchbacks, none too steep. Traverse for a while as the trail becomes overgrown, cross a few small creeks, and follow the route as it becomes fairly steep in spots for the final 6 switchbacks to Oneonta Creek. On the last switchback, or the very first one coming up from Oneonta Creek, is the ¼-mi-long alternate path that keeps you on the E side of the creek to avoid an unnecessary ford during most times of the year. It is well flagged, narrow, and solid, with a few trees and tiny creeks to cross; much work has been done to make the route a fun substitute to becoming soaked or falling in the creek and possibly getting hurt. It ends at the highest footbridge that crosses to the W side of Oneonta Creek. If the water level is low enough to walk over the rocks, or if folks need to cross the creek, however, some will use the larger boulders above or even that big tree high over the water, but I can't recommend this strategy under nearly all conditions. It would be better to take the alternate path down, cross the footbridge W, and ascend less than ¼ mi.

Once directly across Oneonta Creek, walk past the campsite up to the juncture immediately, where turning left (SW) takes you to Franklin Ridge, Multnomah Creek, Bell Creek Trail, or Larch Mountain, and to the right (NW) is the easier Oneonta Trail. Walk down right and soon cross the footbridge back to the E side of the creek, and then follow the emerald forest and thick jungle 1¼ mi to the bridge and waterfall above Triple Falls. Remain on the W side of the creek 1½ mi past Triple Falls down to the final switchback, where you turn right (opposite Trail 400, signed) ¼ mi to the HCRH without difficulty. Finish to the right (E) ½ mi on the wide paved trail to your vehicle at Horsetail Falls TH.

14 NESMITH POINT

ELEVATION: 3872 ft, with 3732 ft vertical gain

DISTANCE: 5¼ mi up, 10½ mi round-trip; 14 mi round-trip loop with Oneonta Gorge

DURATION: 2½–3 hours up, 5 hours round-trip; 6–7 hours round-trip loop with Oneonta Gorge

DIFFICULTY: Mix of strenuous (grueling, steep, narrow path, rocky, overgrown, few rewards) and very challenging (very long loop, route-locating, steeper)

TRIP REPORT: For the loop, leave a shuttle vehicle or bicycle at either John B. Yeon TH for a counterclockwise loop or at Oneonta TH (slightly safer from break-ins and theft) for a clockwise loop, as THs are 4 mi apart using the HCRH and Frontage Road. This trail has decent vertical and is fairly popular with hikers who prefer this type of punishment during spring months in preparation for

Rock of Ages Ridge from Nesmith Point on a snowy yet sunny day!

the more momentous treks when snows melt higher up in the Cascades. No fee or restroom. The completed segment of the HCRH State Trail links John B. Yeon TH to Moffett Creek and benefits hikers and bikers traveling to Cascade Locks from Troutdale and Portland without being forced to utilize the more dangerous Interstate while using several miles of the HCRH and the HCRH State Trail.

TRAILHEAD: John B. Yeon State Park. Take I-84 E from the Portland/Vancouver area to exit 35 (Dodson/Ainsworth), turn left (E) 200 ft toward Warrendale, then right immediately toward Dodson (before the on-ramp), and left (E) again on Frontage Road 2 mi to John B. Yeon State Park on the right. From Hood River or The Dalles, take I-84 W to exit 37 (Warrendale), turn left briefly under the Interstate bridge, and turn left (E) on Frontage Road less than ½ mi to the TH on the right before the on-ramp.

ROUTE: Walk up the visible switchback to the left at the water tower, and turn right in 50 ft onto Nesmith Point Trail 428 for an easy mile through the woods winding S to the junction with Gorge Trail 400. Most of the 2½ mi of Trail 400 from Ainsworth State Park to John B. Yeon State Park was destroyed in a 1996 landslide with flooding, even though a partially cairned route attempts to close the gap through the hilly, moss-covered rock field (frustratingly at that), and so this stretch of the abandoned Gorge Trail is absolutely not recommended. Continue left (E) instead on Trail 428 (unsigned junction) near the creek and up the immediate switchback to a steep traverse along the sometimes uneven rock-embedded trail with good shots of Beacon Rock, Hardy Ridge, and Hamilton Mountain across the river, then along a much steeper, narrower section S for 2 mi and almost 30 switchbacks. Cross the slender NE ridge (2800 ft) of Nesmith Point (with a shot across McCord Creek to Wauneka Point), where the path provides better walking 1½ mi SW up to the Nesmith Point Road 222 intersection.

Turn right (N) to head ¼ mi to the summit up the easy grade with wider terrain. A flattened old outhouse is a landmark near the fairly lackluster destination, which is technically the top of the mountain. See out to nearby Rock of Ages Ridge and the western Gorge. A fairly solid path for those curious continues steeply down N less than ¼ mi and forks right and left near the edge of the cliff band. The right fork quickly vanishes to a complete bushwhack down the NE ridge, and the left fork moves briefly to another look at the Gorge and more of Mount St. Helens. Hike back to the top and descend more established trails more easily for a short while. You may even notice better vistas while hiking down if you are awake to it. Palmer Peak (4010 ft) is 1 mi S of Nesmith Point on Nesmith Point Road 222, as you would drop almost 350 ft to the saddle and then easily bushwhack to the top with decent views if it were legal and not within the Bull Run Watershed boundary. Please avoid this illegal spur as you could put the valuable watershed at risk with a possible land- or rockslide. You would pass Moffett Creek Trail 430 just S of the saddle, which moves left (E) toward Wauneka Point or Tanner Creek. Return the same way instead down Nesmith Point Trail.

Part of the grandiose view between Nesmith Point and Yeon Mountain on Horsetail Creek Trail.

For the long loop with Oneonta Gorge, walk from the summit down Nesmith Point Road past Nesmith Point Trail on the left to the nearby Horsetail Creek Trail 425 turning right (W). Take it easily, enjoying a wonderful panorama of the Cascade Volcanoes and the Columbia Gorge for part of the 1½ mi to the Rock of Ages Ridge juncture and signage. Here you will choose between hiking fairly straightforwardly more than 7 mi down Oneonta Gorge or hiking much, much more steeply slightly more than 3 mi to the right (NW) down Rock of Ages Ridge Trail to Horsetail Falls TH. *See* hike 13 for both descriptions.

15 ELOWAH FALLS TO UPPER McCORD CREEK FALLS

ELEVATION: 500 ft or so, with around 400-plus-ft total vertical gain for both falls

DISTANCE: More than 1 mi to Upper McCord Creek Falls; less than 1 mi to Elowah Falls alone; only 3 mi round-trip for both waterfalls combined

DURATION: ½ hour one way to either of the falls, 1-1½ hours round-trip for both waterfalls

DIFFICULTY: Easiest. Simple, evident, narrow next to a cliff for a time, short hill for both brief strolls

Upper McCord Creek Falls slows to only the right side by autumn.

TRIP REPORT: A generous spring flow slows to a trickle by autumn for both falls. No fee or restroom.

TRAILHEAD: John B. Yeon State Park. *See* hike 14 for directions.

ROUTE: Turn left (E) at the nearby switchback and water tower on Gorge Trail 400 less than ½ mi to an unsigned junction. Leave the easier trail for Upper McCord Creek Falls at a wooden post on the right to hike up switchbacks S, then E, along a narrow cliff band with a guardrail and better-than-average

The mystical approach to Elowah Falls.

views of the Gorge, Beacon Rock, Hamilton Mountain, Mount Adams, and Elowah Falls in the basalt-lined amphitheater. The 64-ft, double-sided Upper McCord Creek Falls is up around the corner and is close enough to be part of the lower falls on the same creek but gets its own name. Only one side runs by the end of summer. The thin trail above the Upper falls ends in a few hundred feet next to the creek. Some folks cross the narrower creek section here or just above the falls with potentially high water to climb the ultra-steep ridge to Wauneka Gap or Wauneka Point, and even fewer people bushwhack with much difficulty to the right of the creek up the precipitous NE ridge of Nesmith Point.

Return carefully more than ½ mi back down to Gorge Trail 400 from Upper McCord Creek Falls, and turn right (E) almost ½ mi effortlessly down 6 switchbacks to the base of the exquisite Elowah Falls near the footbridge over the creek. Watch for the spray that frequently peels away from the narrow 213-ft falls, nailing you in the large alcove as you pass. This could be an enjoyable experience with the full heat of summer bearing down, but otherwise not so much! Walk back the same way on Trail 400 a few feet after crossing the bridge.

ELEVATION: 3120 ft on Wauneka Point; 3725 ft at the S end of Nesmith Point Trail; 3300 ft at the S end of Wauneka Point Trail; with vertical gains of 3000 ft to Wauneka Point most directly, 3840 ft for a loop with Nesmith Point Trail, and 3415 ft for a loop with Munra Point

DISTANCE: 2¾ mi up, 5½ mi round-trip; 11½ mi round-trip clockwise loop with Nesmith Point Trail; 13 mi round-trip counterclockwise loop with Munra Point

DURATION: 2 hours up, 3 hours round-trip; 4–5 hours one way to the highest areas, 6–8 hours round-trip for the loops

DIFFICULTY: Mix of very challenging for most routes (extremely steep bushwhack to Wauneka Gap and beyond, narrow ridge, drop-offs, trail-finding mandatory, exhaustive loop with Nesmith Point Trail) and expert-only (for the loop with Munra Point due to route-finding and steep pitch, which will be somewhat less difficult hiking directly up to Wauneka Point first and then continuing with a long loop to either Munra Point Trail or Nesmith Point Trail)

Wildflowers just above Wauneka Gap.

TRIP REPORT: A low flow on McCord Creek would be helpful when crossing—consider wearing waterproof shoes. If the trails are too wet, access might be nearly impossible for all routes except from Nesmith Point Trail, but then you would have to return by that same route, making for a punishing 18-mi day.

Begin and end all loops from this main TH too. You could also skip Wauneka Point or the loops for Wauneka Gap (at 1600 ft) halfway up and call that your destination for a somewhat less agonizing, shorter day (almost 4 mi round-trip), and return by the same route. No fee or restroom.

TRAILHEAD: John B. Yeon State Park. *See* hike 14 for directions.

ROUTE: Wauneka Point is tough to get to no matter what route you choose. Keep in mind that USGS topographic maps and others are wrong as to the trail placement and even Wauneka Point's true location. Since the route is actually more difficult and confusing to descend (believe it or not), all loops should travel up in this direction to get a feel for the trail. The most direct route is fairly short and is one of the most challenging bushwhacks in the entire Gorge! See and get to Upper McCord Creek Falls (hike 15) and cross the wide creek within the first 50 ft of the top of the falls for your best chance. You can also cross to the E side over logs up a couple hundred feet farther if the water is too high. Come back down the other side with some difficulty to find the faint trail nearest the creek, which traverses N up through the woods steeply a few hundred feet more directly to the bottom section of the ridge proper. This will follow a cliff band to begin and soon becomes more apparent.

There are not enough trail markers or flags to follow, so stay near the thin ridge or dip just right (S or W) when in doubt. There is a visible flagged "route" to ignore, however, which leaves the ridgeline near the bottom at 1000 ft and traverses left (N), then very steeply and roughly through thick flora and trees with no trail down to the old picnic tables just E of Elowah Falls on Gorge Trail 400. That semi-confusing bushwhack also climbs SE, then S, very steeply through the thick woods, and up the scree and moss-covered loose rocks to the top of Wauneka Gap. It is not recommended for most.

Climb the ultra-steep slope and ridge up the main trail, Wauneka Point Trail 429, E more than ½ mi from McCord Creek as the scenery begins to unfold from the rocks below Wauneka Gap. Hike very steeply and carefully up the mostly treeless W fin of the gap on the ridge crest itself or just below it to the right (W) to the top. Note the immense sheer cliff E of the gap while you hike over the lower cliff band and creep past the solo tree clinging onto the ridge coming down briefly to the top of the horseshoe. This may be the end of the hike for folks who have clearly had enough for one day already! There are glorious views of Mount Adams, Table Mountain, Greenleaf Peak, and the Gorge from the top of Wauneka Gap. If you descend by this route, remember to stay nearest the ridgeline or to the left (W) and more toward McCord Creek all the way to the creek crossing.

Continue attentively SE up the super-steep ridge track less than ½ mi as the ridgeline begins to widen. There is one eyeshot coming up almost straight

Mount Adams and the Gorge from Wauneka Point.

down to the Interstate far below. Then follow the faint to disappearing trail S for ½ mi more over a better grade well right (W) of the ridge itself to avoid thick brush and trees. The trail will become more defined with other paths that join it back to the ridge where you cross a scree field and move E of the ridge crest to stay on the proper trail (and soon past 2 actual cairns at the S end of the talus). This rocky opening before and below the cairns comprises Wauneka Point in the center of the high ridge. Scramble 75 ft to the top of the curious old vision quest pits that line the rows of boulders on Wauneka Point and have a nice picnic. There's a respectable shot of Nesmith Point to the W and the whole Gorge below from the rocky hilltop and clearing.

Return the same way or continue S on Wauneka Point Trail 429 for the demanding loops. The trail up is slightly rough to begin with but becomes more pronounced along a superb ridge section, providing the best walking all day over better terrain with limited views 2 mi to its end in the rhododendrons with the Wauneka Point Trail sign standing (was lying down for years) at the juncture with Moffett Creek Trail 430. Pass a small bump (3394 ft) to the left (E) easily within the first mile along the way to the juncture.

To hike down Nesmith Point Trail 428 (straightforward steep trails) from the top end of Wauneka Point Trail, turn right (W) 1½ mi on Moffett Creek Trail without difficulty, working down and then up a bit to Nesmith Point Road 222. Turn right (N) for ½ mi on Nesmith Point Road 222, passing Horsetail Creek Trail 425, which heads left (W) a couple hundred feet before you and Nesmith Point Trail turn right (E, then N) 5 mi down steadily and very steeply with more than 30 switchbacks to the TH.

To hike down the gnarly ridge and most difficult option to Munra Point and beyond from the top of Wauneka Point Trail, continue left (SE) on the primitive Moffett Creek Trail for ½ mi, crossing Moffett Creek halfway, and then head up to the power line opening and intersection. Leave the soon-to-be-rougher Moffett Creek Trail (descends many steep switchbacks for a couple miles to a mandatory ford over Tanner Creek) and follow the power line instead on Talapus Ridge Road 104 down to the left (NE) for 1½ mi over a wide, easy grade in and out of the trees effortlessly (unless there's snow lingering into May), with a very good look of Mount Adams for much of it. Walk left (N) at the last huge tower before the power lines drop into Tanner Creek at about 3040 ft. Here you will have direct views of Tanner Butte and Mount Hood to the SE.

Contour N along a fat ridge section for ½ mi on the barely discernible path through the woods, staying farthest to the right (E, closer to Tanner Creek) to avoid much underbrush, and arrive back at 3040 ft again. Enjoy pleasant hiking down the solid trail momentarily to a major crux that moves down from 2760 ft to 2560 ft in elevation. The route will be abnormally steep for ¼ mi, and the down-climb will be better 30–50 ft E of the ridge crest as ultra-steep, moss-covered boulders block a chunk of the ridge. It's like Ruckel Ridge on steroids and is not recommended for most! Don't drop too far from the ridgeline, however, even if it may be tempting on narrower animal paths. Work yourself back over to join the steep ridge with minimal bouldering for the bottom 50 ft or so on the faint trail.

It's another 2 mi N on the more decipherable route to Munra Point, the first half of which varies in steepness. Then it's a cakewalk to Munra Point, with a little exposure near the rocky outcrops close to the point. Take heed: super-wet or snowy conditions will make this last part all but impossible to cross, as you must traverse a steep slope W of the rocky fin just S of Munra Point. *See* Munra Point (hike 17) for the description 1½ mi down the remainder of the ultra-steep ridge, as you're not quite finished with the taxing slope, and turn left (SW) at the bottom of the unmaintained trail onto Gorge Trail 400. Walk down to cross Moffett Creek immediately, and head up to the HCRH State Trail, taking it left (SW) to parallel I-84 more than 1½ mi without any more difficulty to John B. Yeon TH. There's also an enjoyable option to visit Elowah Falls on Trail 400 up to the left at a large sign in almost ½ mi indicating the falls are "0.4 mi" away. Finish less than a mile past the footbridge below the photogenic falls up switchbacks, then more easily to the TH on the Gorge Trail.

17 | MUNRA POINT

ELEVATION: 1814 ft, with 1764 ft vertical gain

DISTANCE: 3 mi up, 6 mi round-trip from Wahclella Falls TH

DURATION: 1½–2 hours up, 3 hours round-trip

DIFFICULTY: Very challenging. Slender ridge at times, some exposure, super-steep, brief scrambling

Wafer-thin high ridge to Munra Point.

TRIP REPORT: Cold in winter through early March with several feet of snow possible, including drifts near the top (watch for cornices). Sunny with wildflowers in early May and enjoyable most of the summer without much traffic. Rain or a wet trail won't work here, however, because of the steep pitch. *See* hike 16 for a seriously difficult loop connecting the ridge above Munra Point with Nesmith Point Trail or Wauneka Point Trail. Northwest Forest Pass or $5 fee required at Wahclella Falls TH, and there is a portable outhouse.

TRAILHEAD: Take I-84 to exit 40 (Bonneville Dam) and turn S for ¼ mi to the Wahclella Falls tiny parking lot on Tanner Creek. Alternatively you can take I-84 E from Portland and park off the shoulder of the Interstate under the second big brown sign for exit 40 ("Fish Hatchery Sturgeon Cntr exit 40") next to an overgrown driveway just W of the big sign; the early bird will get one of only a couple of spots. Or take I-84 W from Hood River and carefully exit the highway to the left at Moffett Creek immediately W of the bridge with no off-ramp or much room to slow down, precisely across from the milepost 39 marker, onto a short driveway with a gate (room for a half-dozen vehicles without blocking the gate).

ROUTE: From the official TH, backtrack toward the Interstate and walk left (W) on Gorge Trail 400, soon crossing over Tanner Creek Bridge, and proceed S steeply up a little hill and then 1½ mi SW very easily to the narrow trail on the left (S) just E of Moffett Creek. If you don't mind parking next to the busy Interstate, you'll save about 2½ mi round-trip of boring walking parallel to the Interstate as you walk 100 ft up the access driveway to Gorge Trail 400 and turn right (SW) ½ mi to the Munra Point Trail on the left. For those who parked at milepost 39 from I-84 westbound, follow the paved HCRH State Trail right (S) under the Interstate bridge toward the white guardrails, but turn left (NE) onto Trail 400 over the Moffett Creek Bridge and walk up briefly to the Munra Point Trail on the right (only ¼ mi from the gate). There's a "trail not maintained" sign on a tree with "Munra" scratched in underneath 50 ft up from Trail 400.

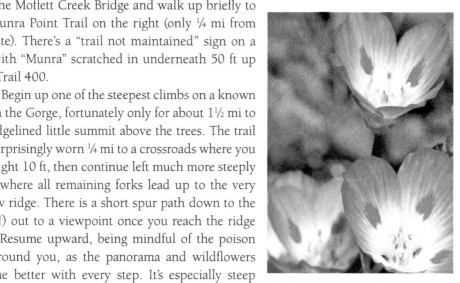

Begin up one of the steepest climbs on a known trail in the Gorge, fortunately only for about 1½ mi to the ridgelined little summit above the trees. The trail E is surprisingly worn ¼ mi to a crossroads where you turn right 10 ft, then continue left much more steeply ¼ mi where all remaining forks lead up to the very narrow ridge. There is a short spur path down to the left (N) out to a viewpoint once you reach the ridge crest. Resume upward, being mindful of the poison oak around you, as the panorama and wildflowers become better with every step. It's especially steep and fun before the top, as you must scramble the looser rock 100 ft up just left (E) of the cliffy ridge-line, hanging on to whatever you can for help. Follow a switchback above this area that heads back to the more solid, superthin ridge above most of the trees.

Clarkia amoena, **or farewell-to-spring, among several wildflowers along the steep ridge to Munra Point.**

There are some intimidating drop-offs along the high ridge, but it's not as steep and the rock is more solid to the nearby point. Carefully scramble more steeply straight up the last 10 ft or proceed left (N) below the petite summit block on the path around and out to a lookout of Bonneville Dam. Munra Point's pinnacle on the open ridge above the highway provides some of the most exceptional views of the Gorge without having to climb 3000–4000 ft or take all day.

ELEVATION: 300 ft, with 250 ft vertical gain

DISTANCE: 1 mi up, 2 mi round-trip

DURATION: ½ hour up, 1 hour round-trip

DIFFICULTY: Easiest. Wide, family-friendly, fleeting

Wahclella Falls past Munra Falls is worth the brief jaunt.

TRIP REPORT: Runoff is good year-round, but spring might prove the best season to visit these falls. Combine this hike with one of the surrounding hikes or other waterfalls in the area. A Northwest Forest Pass or $5 fee is required, and there is a portable outhouse.

TRAILHEAD: Take I-84 to exit 40 (Bonneville Dam) and turn S for ¼ mi to the Wahclella Falls tiny parking lot on Tanner Creek.

ROUTE: Continue S from the parking area on Wahclella Falls Trail 436 for ½ mi on the E side of Tanner Creek. Come around the corner near the beginning and cross the bottom of Munra Falls (a 68-ft sliding cascade down steep-sloping rock) over the bridge. Walk up to the short loop trail around Wahclella Falls, and turn right (W) on it across the creek for a slightly more interesting approach to the footbridge below the 2-tiered, 127-ft falls. The moss-lined rock with a pool at the base of the falls sets the scene quite nicely. Return to the TH without difficulty down the E side of the creek and steeper trail.

ELEVATION: 2760 ft at the high intersection with Wauna Point Trail; 2085 ft at Wauna Point, with 3285 ft vertical gain including 675 ft coming back up from Wauna Point

DISTANCE: 6 mi one way, 12 mi round-trip

DURATION: 3 hours one way, 5–7 hours round-trip with breaks

DIFFICULTY: Very challenging. Steady, super-steep last ¾ mi, very narrow ridgeline to end of point (which some people avoid), some exposure

The versatile Gorge Trail helps link many loop hikes on their bottom portions.

TRIP REPORT: Wear long pants to negotiate tight bushes near Wauna Point in high summer. A GPS device wouldn't hurt either but isn't necessary. This hike is not to be confused with Wauna Viewpoint Trail 402, which is much lower, directly below Wauna Point to the N; that disappointing hike is not mentioned here, as it ends under huge buzzing power lines and is not far enough from the highway noise where you would encounter okay but not outstanding views of the Gorge. A 12½-mi loop without dropping all the way to Wauna Point gets honorable mention, as you would stay on Trail 401 from Trail 401D to Tanner Cutoff Trail 448 steeply down W to Tanner Creek with several little waterfalls, then you would follow Trail 777 N to finish. *See* the maps (pps. 93, 94) and below. No fee. There is a portable outhouse at nearby Wahclella Falls TH. For better facilities, turn N toward the Columbia River after exiting the Interstate, following signs to the Interpretive Center at the Bonneville Fish Hatchery—a noteworthy day trip on its own sans the hiking.

TRAILHEAD: Tooth Rock TH. From Portland, take I-84 E to exit 40 (Bonneville Dam), turn right (S) 30 ft, and then left (E) less than ½ mi up to the Tooth Rock parking lot. From Hood River, take I-84 W to exit 40, turn left (S) under the Interstate, and left (E) just past the on-ramp less than ½ mi up to the Tooth Rock parking lot.

ROUTE: Walk 250 ft W back up the road to the water tower you passed driving to Tooth Rock parking lot, and proceed past the gate and around the turn up Tanner Creek FR-777 for almost 200 ft. Take the short, narrow access trail to the right (SW) for 150 ft, ending at Gorge Trail 400 (unsigned). From here you could turn right down to the parking for Wahclella Falls momentarily, but turn left (E) instead up 2 switchbacks and steadily for a mile to meet FR-777 again. This will be at the second quick pass under huge power lines, with the Interstate sounds dissipating. Directly after passing under the first power lines, trails converge in the woods; simply stay straight to remain on Trail 400 to the next immediate juncture under the same power lines in the next clearing. Turn right and hike SSW on the wide rocky trail back into the woods to stay on FR-777 for an easier mile. You will begin to hear Tanner Creek far below as you walk SE to Tanner Butte Trail 401 and a sign at about 1180 ft on a corner of the old road.

Turn left (E) on Trail 401, crisscrossing a decent-sized creek feed without difficulty for around ¼ mi. A couple of cute little waterfalls appear instantly. Turn S, rising above the side creek for 2 mi with a dozen switchbacks and turns, to the apex of the hike in the woods at 2720 ft. There are some fairly impressive Douglas firs, and the flora is a typical Oregon emerald up the narrower, steady trail as you cross quickly under power lines 2 more times. Notice the view to the W toward the treeless Munra Point, and work to the uppermost area and fairly level ground through a small nondescript campsite. Continue straight near the very

old "trail not maintained" sign on the tree after the camp on Wauna Point Trail 401D, which soon heads left (N). This is opposite the continuation of Tanner Butte Trail 401 from the campsite, which moves right (SE, then S) through tighter trees and then by the information-free brown box on a tree ahead to the more pronounced trail.

The path out to the point is less traveled but stress free to follow, at least for about ½ mi to a faint juncture, where continuing right a few hundred feet on the little spur path toward the ridge crest would give you an alright look at Mount Adams, Mount Rainier, and the top of Mount St. Helens, with the river below. Head left (W) from the spur path instead for ¼ mi, where the trail becomes a bit steeper and curves around E traversing a particularly steep slope the final hundred yards back to the

Several lovely smaller falls line the side creek near FR-777.

Wauna Point to Table and Greenleaf Mountains with Bonneville Dam below!

ridge crest. The route becomes much steeper, then narrower, for a long ¼ mi N to the point. Some people turn around from a little saddle with good-enough vistas before the thicker brush leads somewhat precariously to a small tree-covered bump above Wauna Point.

Splendid panoramas await those who make the effort to hike to the N side of the bump but from a somewhat safer distance than continuing down. For more courageous types, proceed N sensibly as far as you wish, as the views only become more fabulous a couple hundred yards down to the very tip of the point and a grassy flat landing where there are giant drop-offs on three sides. The exposure is pretty exciting indeed. Bonneville Dam is directly below, with Table Mountain and Greenleaf Peak across the Columbia River (Greenleaf Falls between them), and Bridge of the Gods is to the E, with Mount Adams above. The whole Ruckel Ridge loop is also discernible, including the Benson Plateau across Eagle Creek to the E. This is certainly one of the most preeminent perches in the Gorge!

Return steeply about a mile back up Trail 401D to the Tanner Butte Trail juncture just past the campsite, and then it's all downhill to the right (W) on Trail 401. Or you could extend the hike by 6 mi with a clockwise loop by ascending about 800 ft more and then turning right (W) on Tanner Cutoff Trail 448 for a long downhill escapade. *See* Tanner Butte (hike 20) for more of the description.

ELEVATION: 4500 ft, with 4500-plus-ft vertical gain

DISTANCE: 9½ mi up, 19 mi round-trip

DURATION: 4 hours up, 7–8 hours round-trip with breaks

DIFFICULTY: Very challenging. Exceedingly long, steady, ups and downs, steeper last ½ mi to summit

Tanner Butte to Mount Hood over Waucoma Ridge.

TRIP REPORT: Go for a solid bluebird day from July through October so that you can take your time. No fee. There is a portable outhouse at nearby Wahclella Falls TH. For better facilities, turn N after exiting the Interstate, following signs to the Interpretive Center at the Bonneville Fish Hatchery.

TRAILHEAD: Tooth Rock TH. *See* hike 19 for directions.

ROUTE: Follow the description for hike 19 for 4¾ mi to the semi-confusing juncture at 2720 ft, where that hike continues straight for a moment, then left (N) down to Wauna Point on Trail 410D. But continue right (S) from the small campsite intersection instead through thicker trees momentarily on Tanner Butte Trail 401 (note an information-free brown box on a tree ahead) up the ridge slightly more than 2 mi through the forest to the next juncture. The faint Tanner Cutoff Trail 448 dives quite steeply right (W) for 3 mi with many switchbacks and small waterfalls down to Tanner Creek Trail 431 (FR-777). Near the creek you would turn right (N) to follow it 3¼ mi much more easily, completing a loop with Trail 401 sans the summit or for a possible return option from Tanner Butte.

Petite Dublin Lake and camp are ½ mi down left (E) on Trail 401B in a hundred feet from the main route on Tanner Butte Trail. Resume 2¼ mi along the ridge or just W, where the views improve but it's a bit overgrown, even going down a couple times before the final ½ mi bushwhack more steeply left to the wide-open summit on Trail 401C (signed). Here you'll see incredible views of Mount Hood and so much more, with tiny Tanner Lake down to the SE.

"Climb the mountains and get their good tidings. Nature's peace will flow into you as sunshine flows into trees. The winds will blow their own freshness into you, and the storms their energy, while cares will drop away from you like the leaves of autumn."

—JOHN MUIR

21 | EAGLE CREEK TRAIL TO TWISTER FALLS

ELEVATION: 1200 ft, with 1080 ft vertical gain

DISTANCE: 6½ mi up, 13 mi round-trip

DURATION: 3 hours up, 5 hours round-trip

DIFFICULTY: Strenuous. Fairly long, never steep, rocky, sheer sides next to trail, narrow at times

---

TRIP REPORT: Eagle Creek Trail is one of the most jam-packed trails in the entire Gorge during summer months due to its relative ease for family hiking (even with precarious drop-offs) and its numerous quality waterfalls up a long canyon. Some people shorten the walk to 4½ mi round-trip with a visit to Punch Bowl Falls. A Northwest Forest Pass or fee is required to park. Flush toilets at Eagle Creek Campground are open May through October. There is slightly safer parking and a restroom with a camp host (in summer) at the day-use area ½ mi NW of the TH next to the fish hatchery and off-ramp.

TRAILHEAD: From Portland, take I-84 E to exit 41 (Eagle Creek) immediately after the Interstate tunnel, and turn right (S) ½ mi to the end. From Hood River, take exit 40 (Bonneville Dam) from I-84 W and backtrack E to exit 41.

Morning light breaks through the fog in the majestic woods.

ROUTE: Follow Eagle Creek Trail 440 E of the creek most of the distance to Twister Falls. There are dozens of cascades within the first 2¼ mi to Punch Bowl Falls alone, where some people with smaller children turn around. Follow the creek from the TH, bearing SE for ¼ mi before rising above it more than a mile to Metlako Falls Spur Trail 440A. There is a cabled guardrail and several little bridges to cross along the way. The spur trail to 82-ft Metlako Falls on the right is fairly short and gives you a distant look at the fire hose–type falls up the little canyon.

Clear and colorful water along the moss-lined Eagle Creek Trail.

In ½ mi and just after Lower Punch Bowl Falls (12 ft high and 100 yards down the steep spur path, Trail 440B), turn right ¼ mi down the side trail to the base of Punch Bowl Falls (35 ft high). You can also skip the side trail to see the falls from above on the main trail ¼ mi farther. It's in a picturesque amphitheater—but alas, the best waterfalls are yet to come! In another mile, or "3.2 mi" from the TH according to the sign (plus side trails), you arrive at Loowit Falls, a long pretty ribbon with a small cascade at the bottom (90 ft total). It's visible right from the trail, as are most of the falls. Directly above is High Bridge Falls (15 ft high) and High Bridge ("3.3 mi"). Cross to the W side of Eagle Creek for only a mile to 4½ Mile Bridge as you pass Tenas Camp halfway. There you see multi-cascading Skooknichuck Falls up the valley. Tack on the telephoto lens or scramble the thin path down to the creek bed for a better look.

Enjoy the beautiful creek crossing again to the E side on the main trail, where there are a few more noteworthy waterfall sightings and a side path from Wy'East Camp to Wy'East Falls (160 ft total) at more than 5 mi from the TH. Skip it or hike to this seasonal waterfall with some difficulty by heading E over nearby Wy'East Creek easily, then along a steeper, wetter stretch NE a few hundred feet up the path on the S side of the creek. The moss-lined basalt is the perfect backdrop. After this area is Eagle-Benson Trail 434, turning left very steeply NE for 3 mi up to Camp Smokey near the Benson Plateau.

Next on Eagle Creek is undervalued Grand Union Falls (65 ft high) to the right just before Tunnel Falls at about 6 mi from the TH. Walk behind prominent

The trail next to the top of the dynamic Twister Falls.

Tunnel Falls (165 ft high) through the short rock tunnel and continue carefully along the mossy cliff band. Some people love this waterfall best and even turn around to return from here, but truly the most fascinating of all on Eagle Creek is Twister Falls only a couple hundred feet farther. At 6½ mi (with side trails) from the TH, you arrive to the left of the twisting, cascading 130-ft falls. The moss-lined trail sits right next to the top of the falls, which carve the canyon in dramatic fashion. This makes for a better turnaround spot on Trail 440.

There is another trail junction farther S on Eagle Creek Trail in 1½ mi (Indian Springs Trail 435, which meets PCT 2000 near Indian Mountain or splits and continues as Trail 440 to Wahtum Lake). Lastly you would encounter a respectable ford in 2½ mi from Twister Falls, as the main trail turns into Eagle Tanner Trail 433 traveling W several miles more toward Tanner Butte, with a couple of freshwater springs en route.

ELEVATION: 3720 ft, with about 3800 ft vertical gain including ups and downs

DISTANCE: 4½ mi up Ruckel Ridge to the Benson Plateau, 5½ mi up Ruckel Creek Trail, 10 mi round-trip loop connecting both

DURATION: 5–7 hours round-trip loop

DIFFICULTY: Very challenging. Super-steep, narrow, scrambling, route-finding, brief drop-offs, long, hard on knees

Rock field and cliff band from the trail near the bottom of Ruckel Ridge.

TRIP REPORT: Dryer weather results in much better footing for this hike. Poison oak is common but not unbearable throughout Ruckel Ridge, which is usually climbed as a counterclockwise loop with Ruckel Creek Trail 405, though both directions are enjoyable in their own way. Ruckel Ridge has been overhyped as the most difficult hike in the Gorge: it most assuredly is not and might not even make everyone's top 10 list for overall demanding treks. That said, the loop is not appropriate for novice hikers or anyone who prefers to use trekking poles the entire day. A Northwest Forest Pass or fee is required to park. Restrooms are available (portable outhouses in winter), and there is a camp host in summer.

TRAILHEAD: From Portland, take I-84 E to exit 41 (Eagle Creek) immediately

Animated Ruckel Creek with snow melting fast on the Benson Plateau.

after the Interstate tunnel, turn right (S) 100 ft, and park on the left at the day-use area; or cheat and park ½ mi up from there at the Eagle Creek Campground restroom (closed and gated October through April, check with USFS), following the signage left of the large parking lot. From Hood River, take exit 40 from I-84 W, backtrack E to exit 41, and follow the directions above.

ROUTE: From the lower parking lot at the day-use area, walk 200 ft up the paved road on the left toward the campground and take Gorge Trail 400 (signed) to the left briefly as it curves around and follows some metal fencing. Turn right (SE) at a solid fork and signage (for a counterclockwise loop to begin up Ruckel Ridge) before the trail continues downhill, as you walk beside and then through the campground back to the paved road again. Turn to the right after campsite 5 to the Buck Point Trail 439 sign (¼ mi walking from the lower TH).

From the upper parking option at the campground restroom, walk above campsite 5; although the sign indicates Buck Point is ¾ mi, it's really a little less. Take Buck Point Trail 439 E through the woods, along nearly a dozen switchbacks and turns. The last turns are steeper up through the clearing to the underwhelming but okay Buck Point directly under huge power lines. See Bonneville Dam, Beacon Rock, and a multitude of wildflowers in season throughout the clearing. Back into the trees, walk down right (S) of the ridgeline a bit and begin SE up

Ruckel Ridge Trail. Cross the scree field, steeply switching back 8 times or so N a couple hundred feet up to the left side of the cliff band and boulders in the center of the ridge proper. Work extremely steeply up the thin path in the woods to attain the actual ridge on top of the lowest cliff band you saw from below. It's 1½ mi and about 45 minutes to this point from the lower TH.

Proceed up the thin ridge and trail fairly steeply, and stay on or very near the crest even when in doubt for 3 long miles more to Benson Plateau. Follow the ridgeline SE, already using your hands for balance over the basalt boulders, as limited views to the Gorge occasionally materialize through the trees. At around 3 mi from Eagle Creek Campground you arrive at an even narrower ridge section known as the Catwalk at about 2650 ft. Begin up the steep, moss-covered boulders directly on the ridge itself or take the thin bailout trail (which may actually be more difficult) to the right (S) of the ridge if you're afraid of heights. The rocky spine in the woods only lasts for about a hundred yards as you weave your way by a few small trees. Drop-offs of 30–40 ft become apparent and the ridge narrows to the top and end, where you climb down the final large rocks mindfully and wish that section were longer as it really is a lot of fun. In fact the whole ridge is fun, with many micro-breaks in the pitch, including one immediately from the top of the Catwalk heading right and down to a small saddle. Hike left back up to the ridge crest without difficulty ¼ mi or so before the final ¼ mi ENE to Benson Plateau becomes super-steep over a widening ridgeline through slender old-growth pines. You finally near the apex of the climb and level out in the tight forest around 3720 ft.

Meander ¼ mi NNE much more easily through the thinning woods toward the creek on the Benson Plateau. Snowpack here during a "normal" year lingers longer than most locals would probably like, but it's usually gone by July. Thanks to climate change and drought, however, snow may be completely gone by the first week of April if it even snows at all in the Gorge! (Remember to check online for the most recent trip reports.) The trail thins to Ruckel Creek, and you cross over logs or rocks somewhat interestingly but simply enough to the E side wherever it is feasible.

Climb up N a hundred yards or so from the lovely creek to find Ruckel Creek Trail 405 and turn left (W) on it to stroll a bit before you begin a steep descent 4 mi to the bottom (*see* below for Rudolph Spur alternate loop to the same TH). In the first ½ mi, moving down along the creek on the solid trail, a small rockslide area to the left (S) makes for a nice open area to picnic if the plateau is too wet or snowy. It even has a long cascade coming down Ruckel Creek that you can hear and partially see. The trail soon leaves the creek to travel in the same direction W but above, steeply and down many switchbacks, with better viewpoints of the Gorge and 4 big volcanoes.

Once you are finally down to the HCRH State Trail, check out the falls across

Large Cascade Volcanoes, Stevenson, and the Columbia River from Rudolph Spur Trail.

the paved road or even scramble with some difficulty very steeply down to the left for views from the bottom. Walk left (SW) ½ mi on the road effortlessly and continue left on Gorge Trail 400 up to nearby Eagle Creek Campground or to the day-use area, following the metal fence to complete the loop.

The unreasonably abrupt Rudolph Spur Trail 405D is not recommended for most: at less than 3 mi long, it is among the steepest bushwhacks in the Gorge. The few who attempt it usually hike upward, as trail-finding coming down is a bit more confusing, and with snow or a wet trail the route becomes very difficult to negotiate. Loops to the same TH (Eagle Creek, Cascade Locks, or Herman Creek) without a shuttle vehicle will range from 12–14 mi and take about 8–9 hours.

For the speediest descent from Benson Plateau, leave Ruckel Creek Trail in the woods the moment it begins heading downhill (W) on the counterclockwise loop and walk right (N) onto the thin path at the fork over a wide ridge section. Minimal flagging may help as the main path begins off to the right (heading NE, then N) well below the E side of the ridgeline to traverse back to it in about a mile. A tougher but shorter choice is to bushwhack straight down the center of the ridge, where there is no trail, and stay on it when it becomes a super-steep, slick scree field with tiny pebbles. Meet the main traverse path coming from the right at a cairn, and immediately drop from a ledge and flat spot with pleasing views outward.

Continue down the center quite steeply, eventually following the ridge trail even more steeply and more westerly ½ mi toward Rudolph Creek through the trees to near the bottom. Hike N steeply in the forest and down to the right of a downed tree with old notches cut into it (still an okay landmark), then turn more ENE for a mile, crossing talus and continuing steeply down, up, and down the thin and bumpy trail. Even the bottom portion of Rudolph Spur Trail tests your patience and fortitude. You finally descend the emerald forest thick with underbrush and twist down a mellow section to the PCT about 10 ft W of old Dry Creek Road near the creek and a PCT footbridge. The Pacific Crest Trail (PCT 2000) runs from Canada to Mexico for around 2650 mi! Turn left instead for almost 2 mi, crossing a power line halfway on PCT 2000, and then cross the gravel road near Cascade Locks to walk Gorge Trail 400 1½ mi (parallels Interstate), including some switchbacks (annoying after a long day's work!) to the paved HCRH State Trail. Turn left on it about a mile, passing Ruckel Creek Trail halfway, then hike left back onto Trail 400 to Eagle Creek Campground or the day-use area.

23 DRY CREEK FALLS LOOP

ELEVATION: 1080 ft at Pacific Crest Falls; almost 900 ft at Dry Creek Falls; with vertical gains of 1100 ft for Pacific Crest Falls, 700 ft for Dry Creek Falls from Bridge of the Gods TH

DISTANCE: 9 mi round-trip loop including Pacific Crest Falls; 2½ mi up, 5½ mi round-trip loop Dry Creek Falls alone using old Dry Creek Road to finish

DURATION: 1½ hours up to Dry Creek Falls, 3–5 hours round-trip, loop or not, for both falls

DIFFICULTY: Mix of easiest (wide, obvious, steady grade, safe, fairly brief) and moderate (for Pacific Crest Falls or Herman Creek Pinnacles, longer, steeper areas, drop-offs)

TRIP REPORT: Despite its name, Dry Creek Falls runs year-round and may even begin up higher out of sight. For a side trip and for more exercise, add the fascinating Herman Creek Pinnacles and Pacific Crest Falls. A Northwest Forest Pass or fee is required at the official TH. Restrooms are present and open all summer.

TRAILHEAD: From Portland, take I-84 E to exit 44 (Cascade Locks) and follow the exit ramp under Bridge of the Gods, where you turn right and park up at Bridge of the Gods TH in the center of the circle at Toll Gate Park, or just below where there are a few spots, or nearby on city streets when the TH is closed in winter (*see* below for alternate TH). From Hood River and points E, take I-84 W to exit 44 and continue 1¼ mi SW through the town of Cascade Locks on Wa Na Pa Street (US-30) to Bridge of the Gods TH on the left, then turn right in the center of the circle.

Dry Creek Falls in the basalt-lined amphitheater near Cascade Locks.

ROUTE: From Bridge of the Gods TH, take PCT 2000 across the road in the circle NE to parallel the Interstate a couple hundred yards, and then turn right (S) under the bridge. Follow the signage on SW Moody Avenue for another hundred yards or so as the pavement turns to gravel. This is the alternate and winter TH option, with only a couple of spots; otherwise park off the road where it is legal. The PCT is left of the gravel road (SE) while the narrow Gorge Trail 400 is to the right (SW) of the 2 parking spaces.

It's an easy grade on the PCT for 2 mi through the pleasant forest to Dry Creek Road, the first half being uphill and across a power line service road at the top. Take a quick right onto the road, then left off of it to stay on track. Back into the woods, work down E gradually as the Interstate and train sounds are faintly heard to an intersection near the footbridge crossing Dry Creek. Turn right (S) on old Dry Creek Road 211 for ¼ mi more steeply to the end at the falls. At this surprisingly underappreciated (except by locals) destination, the water plunges almost 75 ft over the ledge past the moss-lined columnar basalt in a mostly shady mini-amphitheater.

Back down at the PCT footbridge over the stream, you could extend the hike with a visit to Pacific Crest Falls. These are fine-looking for a smaller waterfall, as they drop a couple times with cascades below them for around 100 ft total give or take, but they slow to a trickle by late summer. You will come back to Dry Creek Road for the loop, but for now cross the bridge and traverse E without difficulty on the PCT (noticing how USGS maps are slightly inaccurate to the falls, but the trail is apparent). Ups and downs are gradual (with the Interstate noise, thankfully, scarcely perceptible) more than 1½ mi through the forest and open scree field to several peculiar jagged basalt fins among the trees known as Herman Creek Pinnacles. Rougher paths make their way left (N) to a more rounded bump, high point (780 ft), and opening in the trees, making for a suitable picnic spot with a nearly 360-degree view to make the jaunt worth it. See a truncated Mount Adams across the Columbia River if it's a clear day. Back on PCT 2000, it's less than ¼ mi farther E easily to Pacific Crest Falls.

Pacific Crest Falls, Dry Creek Falls, and the Pinnacles can also be reached from Herman Creek TH (*see* hike 24). You would follow Herman Creek Trail 406 more than ½ mi up to Herman Bridge Trail 406 E, heading right at the fork opposite the Gorton Creek Trail and Herman Creek Trail. Down at the nearby water, cross the solid bridge over Herman Creek and continue 1½ mi W and S, winding up much steeper turns to the end at the PCT. Turn right (SW) ¼ mi down effortlessly to Pacific Crest Falls on the left, with the Pinnacles soon after on the right (N). Hike about 2 mi down, then left, up to Dry Creek Falls if you're so inclined, and return the same way to Herman Creek TH.

Finish the main route by returning the same way or with a counterclockwise loop by following the sometimes muddy old Dry Creek Road after the footbridge to the right (N) 2 mi down to its end (the top half being quite pleasant, then into pavement on the final turn) at SW Ruckel Street, where you turn left (NW) for ¼ mi passing under the Interstate bridge immediately to its end. Turn right down SW Benson Avenue or SW Adams Avenue to nearby Wa Na Pa Street (US-30), where you turn left (SW) to walk easily through Cascade Locks ½ mi to Bridge of the Gods TH. Please be respectful in the neighborhoods and enjoy the sights. A possible shortcut on the lowest turn of Dry Creek Road before it becomes paved may exist and heads to the right on a traverse at a faint fork (SW) left of the dirt road. Stay S of the Interstate

Pacific Crest Falls in the emerald forest from the PCT.

on a wide bushwhack path with thorny bushes a couple hundred yards to the paved Sternwheeler Drive, which you follow down briefly to meet SW Moody Avenue near the winter TH. Under dry conditions, cheaters can drive up semi-rough Dry Creek Road a mile from SW Ruckel Street (and Cascade Avenue from US-30 in Cascade Locks), park under the power lines, and begin by hiking only a mile easily up FR-211 along Dry Creek to the PCT footbridge.

24 INDIAN POINT LOOP

ELEVATION: 2700 ft on Gorton Creek Trail at the spur trail junction for Indian Point; 2450 ft on Indian Point; 3152 ft for Nick Eaton Way loop; 4050 ft for Casey Creek Trail loop; with vertical gains of 2700 ft, 3162 ft, and 4085 ft

DISTANCE: 4¼ mi one way to Indian Point, 8½ mi round-trip, or round-trip loop with Nick Eaton Way; 12½ mi round-trip loop with Casey Creek Trail

DURATION: 2 hours max to Indian Point, 3–4 hours round-trip or round-trip loop with Nick Eaton Way; 6–8 hours round-trip loop with Casey Creek Trail

DIFFICULTY: Mix of strenuous (near Indian Point or Nick Eaton loop, steeper, switchbacks, long) and very challenging (to Indian Point itself, high exposure, brief, fairly solid, Casey Creek loop excessively steep and fairly long)

TRIP REPORT: Best visited late March through September on bluebird days. If attempting a loop, most people travel clockwise because Gorton Creek Trail 408 is a somewhat more leisurely ascent than the other 2 steep trails from Herman Creek. Hike loops counterclockwise, however, if the super-steep downhill routes seem more taxing. Either way, the loops will be taxing! A Northwest Forest Pass or fee is required, and there is an outhouse. Patrolled and relatively safe from break-ins.

TRAILHEAD: Herman Creek Campground. From Portland, take I-84 E to the Weigh Station exit 1¼ mi past (E of) exit 44 (Cascade Locks) whether open or closed (Department of Transportation office; drive slowly farthest to the left of the Weigh Station island and truck lanes), and merge right on Frontage Road closer to 1½ mi to Herman Creek Campground on the right (sign reads "2 mi"). Return 1½ mi through Cascade Locks on Wa Na Pa Street (US-30) as it becomes the on-ramp to I-84 W. Park at the bottom and walk up the trail less than ½ mi if it's winter or if by chance the gate is locked; otherwise continue to the primary TH by taking the narrow driveway (Herman Creek Road) left of the signed parking at the bottom winding up ½ mi steeply and park at the end near the outhouse. From Hood River and points E, take I-84 W to exit 47 (Herman Creek), continue ½ mi from the off-ramp, take the first left, then turn quickly to the right (SW) on Frontage Road to the nearby TH on the left, and proceed ½ mi left up narrow Herman Creek Road through the trees to the parking by the outhouse.

ROUTE: Take Herman Creek Trail 406 more than ½ mi up 7 quick switchbacks, under a power line more easily, up a couple of longer switchbacks, and then proceed left (E) at a fork with Herman Bridge Trail 406E. Walk more than ½ mi as you fork to the right at a little saddle on the narrowing ridgeline and old roadway

Indian Point towers 2450 feet above the Columbia River.

(Trail 406) to the next major intersection. In the flats at Herman Camp (on the left), Gorge Trail 400 turns hard left (N), Gorton Creek Trail 408 is more in the middle moving E, Herman Creek Trail 406 continues SE with Nick Eaton Way 447 less than ¼ mi farther, and Casey Creek Trail 476 is 2¾ mi farther on Trail 406. Take the middle fork on the signed Gorton Creek Trail, hiking without much difficulty up the steadily steep path for 2½ mi and 10 switchbacks total to the next juncture on a little ridge. The very bottom will be much more abrupt, and you will pass a few huge old-growth Douglas firs with a few peeks out to the

Gorge to the faint 4-way crossing (note that USGS and most other maps are off for this trail and others on the loops).

The Ridge Cutoff Trail 437 takes off right (SSW) quite steeply up to Nick Eaton Ridge. Walk only 50 ft farther on the main trail instead as it begins to descend, and look for the steep narrow spur trail on the left (NE) down to Indian Point. The route becomes clearer but remains very steep ¼ mi out to the point, as you get glimpses of it through the trees before coming down to the rocky protuberance. You will find fantastic Gorge views and room for a picnic from a flat rocky saddle 40 ft before Indian Point. Of course the views are a tad better should you climb up the last 30 ft to the top, but is it worth it? Take your time and watch your contact points (preferably 3) with Mother Earth. The rock is fairly solid on the pinnacle, and it's just as lofty as it appears from all angles, being no more than a few feet wide: be mindful and make no mistakes. Wind Mountain is directly across the river, with Mount Adams standing largely behind, and you see Goat Rocks to Mount St. Helens as well as up and down the Gorge mostly unhindered.

Return up the thin path to the main trail, where you can turn right and head back down W on Gorton Creek Trail as the simplest option. You can also climb up Trail 437 for ¾ mi to Nick Eaton Way (*see* below from Point 3152) for the shorter clockwise loop, or turn left (SE) on Gorton Creek Trail almost a mile a bit downhill narrowly and easily to Deadwood Camp for longer loop options. The best (albeit steeper) one might be just before and W of the camp and Grays Creek to find Deadwood Trail 422 turning sharply right (W) ½ mi rather steeply up to Nick Eaton Ridge (check the map on p. 95 for an even longer but less steep loop option, adding another mile using the rest of Gorton Creek Trail to Nick Eaton Ridge Trail).

From where Deadwood Trail meets the high ridge at completely faded signs, turn left (SE) on Nick Eaton Way (or right ½ mi up to Point 3152 and down Trail 447 for a slightly easier go of it—*see* below) for a mile of ridiculously steep hiking along Nick Eaton Ridge, crossing it a few times, mellowing out, then becoming super-steep briefly to the high point as you descend to the next junction along the narrow, mossy, rock- and tree-covered ridge crest. Turn right (W) at more unreadable old signs, where it's crazy-steep almost 2 mi down Casey Creek Trail, which is unmaintained and thin but obvious as you lose 2480 ft over the span! There are 4 switchbacks near the top and more than a dozen toward the bottom, and that's not nearly enough to prevent the pain in your knees, hips, and ankles—unless you are one of the local deer.

Turn right (NW) at the sweet little established camp and Cedar Swamp sign (pointing left) on Herman Creek Trail for 2¾ mi without any more difficulty back to the beginning of the loop at Gorton Creek Trail. Pass nearby E Fork Herman Creek Falls, a small seasonal cascade on the trail at Camp Creek, and lastly the taller and nice-looking Nick Eaton Falls, which drop over mossy rock. You ascend slightly ¼ mi or so on the widening trail close to the Nick Eaton Way juncture before the main intersection, and then it's only 1¼ mi to the main TH.

From the top of Ridge Cutoff Trail at Point 3152, turn right (W) down Nick Eaton Way as you immediately leave the high ridge, and trudge 2 mi to Herman Creek Trail with a few significant vistas to break the monotony of the never-ending steeper switchbacks. Turn right at the bottom on Trail 406 for 1½ mi NW to the TH without any more trouble, passing the Gorton Creek Trail intersection momentarily.

> **"Today I have grown taller from walking with the trees."**
>
> **—KARLE WILSON BAKER**

25 GREEN POINT MOUNTAIN

ELEVATION: 4737 ft, with 4500 ft vertical gain from the Columbia River

DISTANCE: 10¼ mi up, around 20 mi round-trip with brief loop near summit

DURATION: 5 hours up, 9 hours max round-trip

DIFFICULTY: Very challenging. Longer than most hikes from the Gorge, steep in places, wide ridge

TRIP REPORT: Snow may linger near the top into late June. This summit can be attained considerably closer from Rainy Lake Campground or even Wahtum Lake Campground, but it is not as rewarding unless you begin from the shorter drive to the Gorge TH. A Northwest Forest Pass or fee is required, and there is an outhouse.

TRAILHEAD: Herman Creek Campground. *See* hike 24 for directions.

ROUTE: *See* Indian Point Loop (hike 24) and the map on p. 95 to Ridge Cutoff Trail 437, and take the following trails up and back the same route from the TH for the most efficient choices: Trail 406 to Trail 408 all the way to the summit, or Trail 406 to Trail 408 all the way to Trail 418. Or you could take Trail 406 to Trail

From Green Point Mountain across Rainy Lake to Mount Defiance, with Mount Adams back to the left.

408 to Trail 437 to Trail 447, then hike a painfully steep section S along Nick Eaton Ridge to the Casey Creek Trail 476 juncture at 6 mi from the TH. Continue SE a mile to the end of Nick Eaton Ridge 447 at the Gorton Creek Trail 408 intersection and stay right on Trail 408 S for ¾ mi to the next juncture. Take Green Point Mountain Ridge Trail–Plateau Cutoff Trail left (E on Trail 418) at the sign for a simple little loop around the summit plateau area. After ½ mi, stay right (S, then SW) on Green Point Mountain Ridge Trail 418 for 2 mi more, hiking effortlessly to the peak.

Views on top or along the way are of the Gorge, Mount Adams, North Lake, Rainy Lake, Mount Defiance, Mount Hood, and others. On the return, go left (N) at the fork ¼ mi N of the summit on Gorton Creek Trail for 3 mi (ignoring other trails), then left (NW) on Nick Eaton Ridge Trail for 2½ mi along the narrowing and ultra-steep ridge section. Turn left (W) near Point 3152 and head very steeply and more quickly down Trail 447, saving about a mile, or for an easier option head right (NE) down Ridge Cutoff Trail steeply ¾ mi to Gorton Creek Trail, walk left (W) 2½ mi to the bottom, and finish by turning right 1¼ mi on Herman Creek Trail. Excellent. What a day! What a life!

> **"Only those who will risk going too far can possibly find out how far they can go."**
>
> **—T. S. ELIOT**

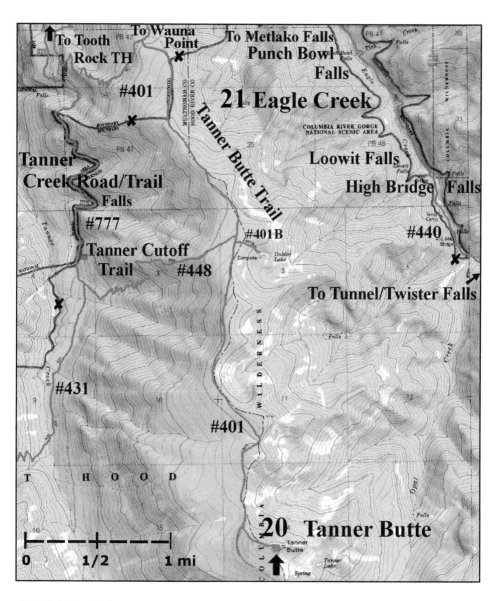

To Tooth Rock TH

To Wauna Point

To Metlako Falls
Punch Bowl Falls

#401

21 Eagle Creek

Tanner Butte Trail

COLUMBIA RIVER GORGE
NATIONAL SCENIC AREA

Tanner Creek Road/Trail Falls

Loowit Falls

High Bridge Falls

#777

#401B

#440

Tanner Cutoff Trail

#448

To Tunnel/Twister Falls

#431

#401

T H O O D

20 Tanner Butte

Tanner Butte

Tanner Lake

Spring

0   1/2   1 mi

COVERS HIKES 19-21

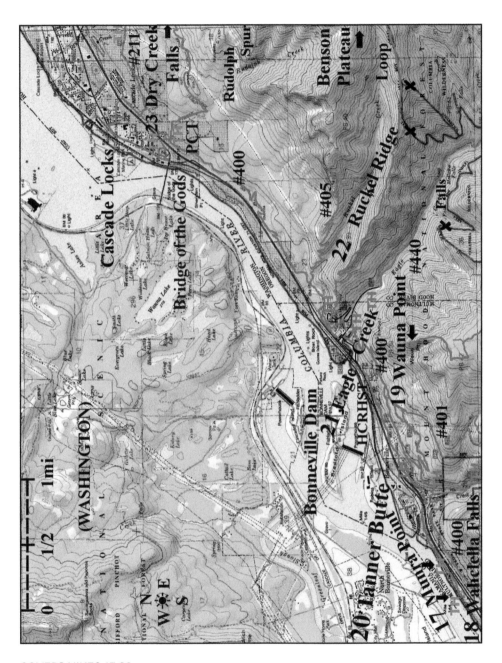

COVERS HIKES 17-23

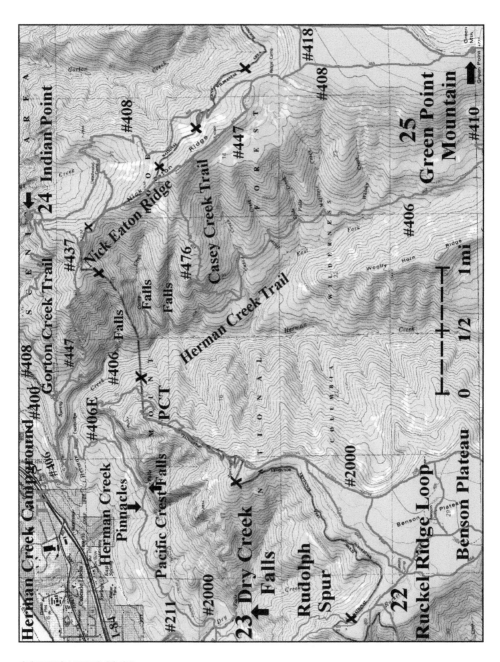

COVERS HIKES 22-25

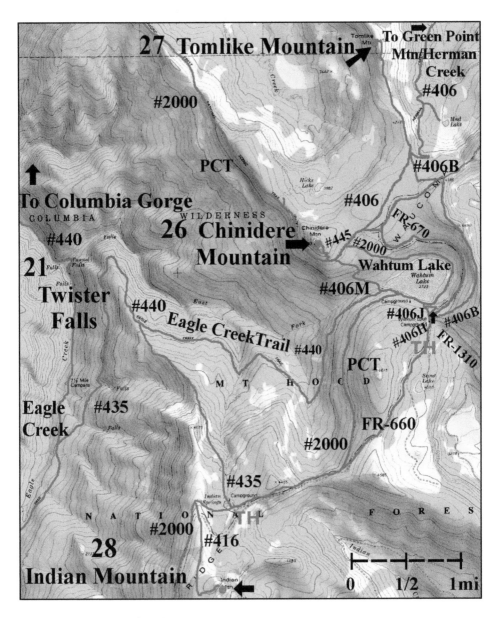

27 Tomlike Mountain

To Green Point Mtn/Herman Creek #406

#2000

PCT

To Columbia Gorge

COLUMBIA

WILDERNESS

#406B

#406

FR-2670

#440

26 Chinidere Mountain

#445 #2000

Wahtum Lake

21 Twister Falls

#440

Eagle Creek Trail #440

#406M

#406J #406B

#406H FR-1310

PCT

Eagle Creek

#435

FR-660

#2000

#435

#2000

28 Indian Mountain

#416

0   1/2   1mi

COVERS HIKES 21, and 26-28

ELEVATION: 4673 ft, with about 1165 ft vertical gain counting all the ups and downs

DISTANCE: 2½ mi one way directly, 5 mi round-trip or round-trip loop with Chinidere Cutoff Trail; 7 mi round-trip loop with Anthill Ridge Trail

DURATION: 1 hour one way directly using Chinidere Cutoff Trail, 2 hours round-trip for the shortest option and 3 hours or more with loops

DIFFICULTY: Mix of moderate (longer on the PCT or FR-670, mostly gradual or flat, steeper to peak) and strenuous (using Chinidere Cutoff Trail, several trail options, narrow, solid, steeper at times)

TRIP REPORT: It is windy on the summit, but bring a picnic and the kids. This popular, nearly year-round playground offers plenty of parking, people, THs, and camping. A Northwest Forest Pass or fee is required, and a pit toilet is present and open all summer. The road is not plowed in winter, therefore you may have to snowshoe up the last mile or so to the TH and beyond from where you can no longer drive.

TRAILHEAD: Wahtum Lake. Take I-84 E to exit 62 (Hood River), turn right on US-30 for 1¼ mi through town, and turn right at the signal onto OR-281 S (13th Street into Tucker Road) almost 5 mi. Cross Hood River by Odell, turn right (SW) to continue past Tucker County Park on OR-281 S (Dee Highway) 6¼ mi to Dee, turn right over the railroad tracks (past an old mill, then over the bridge), and turn left at the signage for Wahtum and Lost Lakes. Stay on Lost Lake Road 4¾ mi, veer right on FR-13 for 4¼ mi toward Wahtum Lake, then veer right on FR-1310 almost 6 mi. Be alert on the narrowing road, and watch for oncoming traffic and natural obstacles. Park in the lot as the pavement ends or along the roadway wisely. Easy 1½ hours from Portland or ½ hour from Hood River.

ROUTE: For the easier counterclockwise loop around the lake, begin to the right down Wahtum Lake Trail 406H less than ½ mi and 1 switchback to PCT 2000. For the easiest route on FR-670 (Rainy-Wahtum Trail to Rainy Lake into Tr 409), stay high at Wahtum Lake TH on the wide old road that continues right around the lake with no elevation change to the short trail left to Herman Creek (*see* the map on p. 96 for this). Turn right from the main route on Trail 406H onto the PCT 1½ mi meandering N around the lakeside through the tall forest with shots

From Chinidere to Tomlike and Mount Adams on a peaceful winter stroll.

of Chinidere Mountain across the water W. The route becomes slightly steeper leaving the lake to the next juncture. Herman Creek Trail 406 moves to the right (N) 2¼ mi to Tomlike Mountain, 1¼ mi to Anthill Ridge Trail 406B, or 10 mi N to Herman Creek Campground in the Gorge. Continue left on the PCT easily more than ¼ mi to Chinidere Mountain Trail 445 at a small sign on the right (N).

The summit trail is a hundred feet past Chinidere Cutoff Trail 406M (left, S) and skirts the ridgeline ½ mi steeply through the trees, finally rising above them through the scree to wind up to the endearing little rocky peak. One short summit loop option, for those who desire a bit more of a challenge, leaves the main trail in the woods left after 5 switchbacks to climb the loose shale path a couple hundred yards even steeper up the last bit of Chinidere's S ridge. It might be better on knees and ankles to save this for the descent. Views of Mount Hood from the top couldn't be better. Tanner Butte is to the W across Eagle Creek, and to the NE is Mount Adams far behind nearby Tomlike Mountain and Wahtum Lake. On a clear day even Mount Jefferson and Mount Rainier can be seen. Simply stunning for relatively minimal effort! Return the same way or try one of a few loops to enrich your day.

For the longer but more scenic and simple Anthill Ridge return loop, head S down the steep open ridge or the main trail in the woods from the summit back to the PCT and turn left (NE) for about ¼ mi, then stay left (NE) on Herman Creek Trail 406. Move past the trail that forks right (E) briefly to old FR-670. That wide old road heads NE ½ mi shorter for the Anthill Ridge loop or right for an even shorter loop directly back to the TH, both of which are rather boring. Walk over more level ground on Herman Creek Trail NE a mile to the N end of Anthill Ridge Trail. Turn right (S) at the tiny 4-way intersection in the woods easily for ½ mi and cross FR-670 at Waucoma Ridge to stay on Trail 406B. Cruise S for 1½ mi up, then down, the delightful Anthill Ridge with decent views, finishing SW below the ridgeline to the TH.

For the slightly more difficult clockwise loop around Wahtum Lake and Chinidere Mountain from the TH, take Wahtum Express Trail 406J (a sign incorrectly calls it Trail 406M) to the left of Wahtum Lake Trail 406H (or take Trail 406H—a tad easier and longer) as you commence down to the lake. Walk almost ¼ mi through the forest very steeply N down several hundred railroad ties made into steps to PCT 2000, and turn left ¼ mi around the S side of the decent-sized colorful lake. See Chinidere Mountain through the big trees and across the water to the NW. Continue right at the fork with the PCT (bearing SW) to stay near the lake now on Eagle Creek Trail 440 a couple hundred yards, then stay right again when Trail 440 continues left (WSW several miles to Eagle Creek). Cross Eagle Creek East Fork now on Chinidere Cutoff Trail 406M (PCT shortcut) over the logjam where it is safe (judiciously with children), and leave the lake immediately to climb NW steeply up ½ mi including left across a nice-looking creek. It's ¼ mi more to the PCT, where you turn left (W) a hundred feet and finish to the right (N) on Trail 445 as above. Return the same way or try one of the clockwise loops above.

27 | TOMLIKE MOUNTAIN

ELEVATION: 4555 ft, with vertical gains of 800 ft with no loop, 1375 ft including a Chinidere Mountain loop

DISTANCE: 3¼ mi up, 6½ mi round-trip; 8½ mi round-trip loop with Chinidere Mountain and Wahtum Lake

DURATION: 1½ hours up, 3 hours round-trip; 4–5 hours round-trip loop with Chinidere Mountain

DIFFICULTY: Strenuous. Steeper areas near the summits, narrow at times, ups and downs, longer loop

---

TRIP REPORT: July through September is best. In winter the road to Wahtum Lake is open but not plowed: you may need to snowshoe in from where you can no longer drive. Only a few hardy souls will hike this peak 20 mi round-trip from the Gorge with a decent ford on Herman Creek Trail 406 or a very rough bushwhack up Woolly Horn Ridge N of the summit. A Northwest Forest Pass or fee is required, and a pit toilet is present and open all summer.

TRAILHEAD: Wahtum Lake. *See* hike 26 for directions.

ROUTE: Take Anthill Ridge Trail 406B across the road from Wahtum Lake Campground behind the outhouse where paths merge. Walk 1½ mi (N) through the woods, gradually gaining 500 ft on the traverse toward Anthill Ridge, then lose about 100 ft as views down to the lake (and of Mount Jefferson in one eyeshot) are revealed at the uppermost part of a few scree fields along the top of the ridge crest. You can also see Mount Hood, Indian Mountain, Chinidere Mountain, and Tanner Butte. Cross FR-670 at Waucoma Ridge (hint: right NE 2¾ mi is Green Point Mountain, and a 2½-mile simple loop option with Rainy Lake) and continue ½ mi W, then N, to a tiny 4-way intersection where Herman Creek Trail 406 turns sharply left (Chinidere Mountain) or hard right (also toward Green Point Mountain, or the Gorge) on the corner, while the unsigned but cairned and obvious path heading straight or slightly right leads 1¼ mi NNW to Tomlike Mountain.

Hike in and out of the low trees on or just E of the wide ridgeline, finally rising above most of the trees as the route becomes steeper through boulders and scree. Finish to the peak with incredible views of nearly all of the mountains between the Columbia River Gorge and the N face of Mount Hood. Return the same way or see Wahtum Lake to Chinidere Mountain (hike 26) and reverse directions from the N end of Anthill Ridge Trail onto Herman Creek Trail to finish with a loop, including Wahtum Lake and/or Chinidere Mountain!

Indian Mountain in the background with Wahtum Lake below from Anthill Ridge.

Last bit to Tomlike Mountain with Mount Hood standing hugely behind.

28 | INDIAN MOUNTAIN

ELEVATION: 4891 ft, with vertical gains of 671 ft from Indian Springs TH and 1393 ft from the more popular Wahtum Lake TH, including 225 ft coming back up from Wahtum Lake by not using nearby FR-660

DISTANCE: 1¼ mi up from Indian Springs TH, 2½ mi round-trip; 3¼ mi up (and return) on old Wahtum Lake Road (FR-660), 6½ mi round-trip; 4¼ mi up from Wahtum Lake Campground by starting down to Wahtum Lake as most people do for this hike, 8½ mi round-trip

DURATION: 1 hour up, 1½ hours round-trip from Indian Springs TH; 1½ hours up, 2½ hours round-trip using Wahtum Lake Road (FR-660); 1¾ hours one way, 3½–4 hours round-trip by Wahtum Lake for the primary route

DIFFICULTY: Moderate. Popular trails, rocky, steeper on the longest route, fairly good signage

TRIP REPORT: The cheating way up FR-660 to old Indian Springs Campground saves time and mileage if you're trying to climb several area summits, or you could walk up the lackluster dirt road (FR-660) from the Wahtum Lake TH. But the route that travels by Wahtum Lake is the most appealing if you're not in a hurry. A Northwest Forest Pass or fee is required, and a pit toilet is present and open all summer.

Down toward Mount Adams on the trail from Indian Mountain.

TRAILHEAD: Wahtum Lake. *See* hike 26 for directions to the principal TH. For the shortest route, continue left onto the dirt road (FR-660) from Wahtum Lake TH for 2 mi SW easily, and stay right of any forks to the end of the drivable road at the gate just past old Indian Springs Campground.

ROUTE: For the shortest walk, jump on PCT 2000 from the abandoned Indian Springs camping area and TH or amble up the road, which quickly meets the PCT heading W ¼ mi easily up to the next junction and sign in the clearing. Leave the PCT for the open ridge hike left (S) on Indian Mountain Trail 416 about a mile to the summit as you pass giant cairns, radio towers (regrettably), wildflowers, and an appealing panorama of a few of Washington's big Cascade Volcanoes, the Gorge, and all the local mountains. It is hard to capture the 360-degree living postcard with a camera, but this high ridge holds a uniquely fascinating perspective encapsulating the Pacific Northwest. The wide path climbs more steeply back into the trees to an old lookout tower foundation within the rock pile on top, with somewhat limited but decent views.

From the main TH at Wahtum Lake Campground, take Wahtum Express Trail 406J (a sign incorrectly calls it Trail 406M) to the left as you begin down to the lake. Walk almost ¼ mi steeply N down several hundred railroad ties made into steps to the PCT, and turn left ¼ mi around the S side of the decent-sized lake with Chinidere Mountain across it to the NW. Turn left (W, then S) away from Wahtum Lake to stay on the PCT with a steady grade through the trees 1½ mi. Then parallel FR-660 for another mile on its right side SW to

Indian Springs Campground as you get an eyeshot of Indian Mountain along the way. Remain on the PCT ¼ mi more W to the summit trail on the left (S) and follow Trail 416 up the ridge as described above.

Look who's not invisible!

29 SHELLROCK MOUNTAIN

ELEVATION: 2093 ft, with 2000 ft vertical gain

DISTANCE: 2 mi up, 4 mi round-trip

DURATION: 2 hours or more up, 3–4 hours round-trip

DIFFICULTY: Very challenging. Scree path, super-steep, bushwhack, becomes overgrown, scrambling, poison oak, no signs, GPS with tracking helpful around summit.

TRIP REPORT: The unmaintained trail to the minor summit used to be fairly obvious before windstorms felled dozens of trees in the fall of 2014, taking out much of the more "popular" route above the mossy rock field. Most people forego the top these days and stop at ½ mi up near an interesting metal staircase leading to better-than-average views, or continue up the switchbacks through the rock field ½ mi farther to the trees before turning around. And for the curious gluttons for punishment there are other ways to the little peak, including a decent bush-whack path a few feet W of the old route.

Expansive views don't happen above the rock field on this scramble, which is usually undertaken for solitude, a bucket list item, a short workout, or all three. More official access and safer parking is forthcoming in 2016 as construction is completed on the HCRH State Trail from a new Wyeth TH (exit 51 from I-84) with a vault toilet, bicycle parking, RV turnaround, picnic tables, and an informative kiosk. The HCRH State Trail will travel (E) right by Shellrock Mountain en route to Hood River and will tack on 2½ easy miles round-trip to the hike when completed. No fee or restroom.

TRAILHEAD: Only accessible from I-84 E, with very limited parking (until 2016). From Hood River and points E, take exit 51 (Wyeth) from I-84 W, then continue on I-84 E as you would from the Portland area (about 9 mi from Cascade Locks), where from Wyeth you immediately see the steep and rocky Shellrock Mountain to the right of the Interstate ahead. Being careful, you must slow down quickly and park off the shoulder of the Interstate to the right as soon as you pass a long retaining wall holding back the mountain. It comes after milepost 52½. A small white sign reading "Property of Dept. of Transportation Highway Division" marks the concealed TH, with only a few parking spots conveniently and fairly safely off the shoulder. Drivers returning W must continue on I-84 E to exit 56 (Viento State Park) to catch I-84 W.

ROUTE: Walk over the guardrail past the little white sign onto the faint, flat trail for only 150 ft E, then you must steadily climb the decently graded scree path and 8 switchbacks up the moss-covered rock field to the right (S). Share part of a mossy old wagon road with original stonework from 1872 on one small stretch. At the top of the last 2 switchbacks and uneven rock trail (½ mi) is a fork at another switchback. To the left (E) is a solid metal staircase, then a cabled hand-

Super-steep mossy boulder field toward Shellrock Mountain.

rail along a narrow section on the continuation of the Backbone Traverse Trail. Views of Dog Mountain are nice and it's worth checking out a few yards beyond the top of the stairs if you wish to investigate, but come back to the switchback at the fork and continue right (W) instead up the mossy opening and 9 more switchbacks (½ mi) to the forest where the true scrambling begins in earnest.

Pay close attention to where the disappearing trail is for the remainder as you squeeze through an opening where a log was cut off the trail but 2 more trees fell on top. Next, an unclear fork covered with branches and blowdowns obscures what used to be the somewhat easier path (toward an old overgrown weather station) more left (S) of and off the narrow ridgeline (closer to another rock field with better views) as shown exed out on the map on p. 110. The horrible unmaintained section covers the entire NE ridge of Shellrock, but is the worst from 920 ft to 1320 ft. To bypass the main ridge for a still very difficult ½ mi up the super-steeps, watch for rock cairns and flagging upward. Climb a few quick rougher switchbacks heading more westerly briefly to an ultra-steep SSW shoulder at a larger cairn. Turn left and follow this narrow spine and shoulder back to the main ridge by ascending the moss-covered steep pitch a hundred yards with no trail. Then the path thins as you continue very steeply before you leave the shoulder left and go between 2 trees with flags tied to both near the NE ridge.

Until volunteer hikers continue to build new trails it's more of a steep bushwhack to finish to the nearby big sleepy summit cairn, with fallen limbs covering most discernible paths to some extent near the widening ridge. There are a few variations within this newer route as of spring 2015; just remember when coming down from the top as some people are pulled N a bit (toward another scramble), but then you must head hard right (E) back to the NE ridge to avoid cliffy areas. This is why tracking trails to a device (or devices) can be key at times. Watch for the flags tied to the trees you go between en route to the ultra-steep shoulder.

The top in the woods holds few rewards. Partial views outward are mostly overgrown and it may or may not be worth it to continue with no trail over the branches and sticks a hundred yards down slightly and up a bump to a couple micro-breaks through the forest. Return the same way, or as close as possible, down to the more manageable switchbacks through the mossy rock field to finish.

ELEVATION: 4959 ft, with vertical gains of 4839 ft for the summit, about 1000 ft for the low waterfall loop without the summit

DISTANCE: 13 mi round-trip clockwise loop with Starvation Ridge Trail; 3 mi round-trip low waterfall clockwise loop

DURATION: 3½–4 hours up, 6–7 hours round-trip loop; 2 hours round-trip low waterfall loop

DIFFICULTY: Mix of very challenging (for the summit, fairly long, steadily steep with micro-breaks, solid trails, demanding) and moderate (for the somewhat family-friendly waterfall loop, quite steep briefly, drop-offs, not long-lasting)

Easy to access **Cabin Creek Falls is still quite good-looking, even though partially blocked at the bottom.**

TRIP REPORT: The Columbia River Gorge's highest mountain close to the river has some serious vertical and much traffic, but surprisingly it is neither the hardest hike in the Gorge nor the prettiest peak with the best views. Multiple communication towers and a rough 4WD road bustling with day-trippers and motorcycles in the summer dominate the sizeable flat summit area. It's a bit nicer without all the people and bugs in late fall or spring, when the road is closed and snow resides at the peak, although route-finding becomes slightly problematic. No fee. Restrooms with flush toilets are present at the main TH and rest area in the Gorge, where wheelchair-accessible and noteworthy Starvation Creek Falls are only 200 ft past the restrooms.

TRAILHEAD: Starvation Creek State Park. From Portland or Vancouver, take I-84 E to exit 55 and park in the small lot at the end of the off-ramp. From Hood River or The Dalles, take I-84 W to exit 51 (Wyeth), then follow I-84 E to exit 55.

Marvelous up or down the narrow crest that is Starvation Ridge.

ROUTE: For both loops, walk ¼ mi W past the sign for Mount Defiance along the Interstate to Starvation Ridge Cutoff Trail 414B on the left (100 ft E of Cabin Creek Falls). Follow it up 7 switchbacks S rather steeply through the woods below a large cliff band with steep terrain around for ½ mi to its end at Starvation Ridge Trail 414. See the top of Cabin Creek Falls through the trees from the top of the switchbacks. For the low loop you'll head to the right, but turn left (NE) first for 150 ft up to a decent look at the Gorge from a tiny cliffy perch left of the trail.

If you've had enough already, you could bail on the more arduous hike for the much shorter, easier waterfall-lined loop by walking back down Trail 414 past Starvation Ridge Cutoff Trail (you just came up) to cross Cabin Creek briefly without difficulty, and stroll NW for ¼ mi up 4 switchbacks under a power line to another shot of the Gorge near a cliffy area off the trail to the right. Climb 2 more turns to a little ridge crest in the clearing, and descend 2 switchbacks to a short spur path heading right to more views, but be careful as the spur terminates suddenly and is literally a dead end! Descend the main trail nearly ½ mi and 4 more switchbacks as you reenter the forest to cross Warren Creek over the logs and boulders wherever possible, using some caution. After one more viewpoint, arrive down at the next junction on Trail 414 less than ½ mi from Warren Creek. Turn left on Mount Defiance Trail 413 instead for a short side trip 200 ft W up to the delightful Lancaster Falls and see the end of this hike to finish.

For the longer and much more difficult trek up to Mount Defiance from the cliffy perch 150 ft above the Starvation Ridge Cutoff Trail juncture on Starvation Ridge Trail, hike more than ¾ mi E up 15 switchbacks under a big power line. You will hike in and out of the woods and through a steep clearing with wildflowers.

Crowd-pleasing Lancaster Falls drapes across the trail.

There's a fleeting look of the parking lot, the Gorge, and neighboring Shellrock Mountain, with Wind and Dog Mountains on the other side of the Columbia River. Now climb S into the woods on the wide trail, without much for views, up the steep and narrow but tremendous Starvation Ridge for a mile. Then there will be one great shot of the Gorge and Mount St. Helens just before it levels out somewhat on the now rockier trail. Head ¾ mi more easily to the left (SE), leaving the ridgeline, and enjoy a sudden full shot of Mount Adams on the traverse up after you pass a huge topless Doug fir with an equally impressive massive curving branch. Ascend 8 switchbacks S through the forest and across the rock field to the end of Trail 414, where the path veers to the right (SW) turning into Mitchell Point Trail 417 for 1½ mi to Warren Lake. The first segment covers about a half-dozen steep switchbacks up to a little saddle, where you stay right at a juncture and barely descend the same trail to the "Gorge-ous" lake! This portion is also known as Warren Lake Trail 417A to Mount Defiance Trail. Get your first good look at Mount Defiance before reaching the water.

The grade is okay ¾ mi W as you wind up above Warren Lake on Trail 417A through the scree (with a sweet panorama of the Gorge, Mount St. Helens, Mount Rainier, and Mount Adams) and then move into the trees to Mount Defiance

Trail 413. Turn left (SW) to finish 1¼ mi to the top, cutting across jeep roads to climb steeply and directly to the summit as all tracks lead to the top. There you will encounter partly obscured panoramas, thanks to trees and radio towers, but Mount Hood looks grand.

Return the same way or walk S from the peak on the continuation of the trail and a somewhat more interesting little loop at the top of the mountain, where the trail quickly curves back around to the right (N), then NE to meet the main summit trail you came up. Stay left (N) on Mount Defiance Trail 4 mi to the bottom to remain on the big clockwise loop. It's painfully steep almost the entire way down the N ridge, but the wide tacky trail makes it easier to jog and keep traction for slowing down for most of it through the thick woods. Descend 25 steep switchbacks to the very bottom, where it makes absolute sense as to why most people take the loop in this direction!

Walk much more easily to the right (E) at the bottom under the power line area, and traverse the slope E down to pass picturesque Lancaster Falls, which precedes the mossy, rock-lined Wonder Creek crossing the trail. Only the last 20 ft of the 303 ft total for this several-tiered waterfall can be seen from this locale. Stay on Mount Defiance Trail almost a mile more to the TH without any difficulty. In ¼ mi you will pass man-made Hole-in-the-Wall Falls as you cross the bridge. (These 100-ft-high, 2-tiered falls are stolen from adjacent Warren Falls, which now only runs after big spring storms at a fraction of its historic levels. However, Warren Falls might be restored to a shadow of its eminent past in the not-so-distant future: the fake falls once diverted water that was destroying the old highway, but now they serve no purpose.) Walk almost ½ mi E to 220-ft, tiered Cabin Creek Falls, which is difficult to see all at once thanks to large boulders at the bottom. Finish about ¼ mi bordering the Interstate to the TH as you pass Starvation Ridge Cutoff Trail. Back at the TH don't forget to visit the taller, more visible, cascading Starvation Creek Falls (227 ft) a few hundred feet up the paved path from the parking lot past the restrooms to the right.

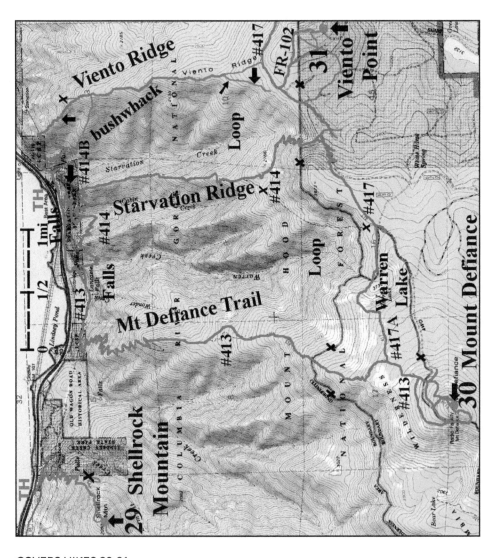

COVERS HIKES 29-31

31 | VIENTO POINT LOOP

ELEVATION: 3560 ft, with 3440 ft vertical gain

DISTANCE: 4½ mi up one of two long ridges to the point, 9 mi round-trip clockwise loop with Starvation Ridge Trail

DURATION: 5–6 hours round-trip clockwise loop to the same TH

DIFFICULTY: Very challenging. Consistently steep, narrow but workable and rewarding ridges, bushwhacking mandatory on Viento Ridge, peaceful, GPS device helpful

TRIP REPORT: Leave the crowds lumbering up to Mount Defiance for this lost but not forgotten little treasure for those willing to push it! Hike in either direction but coming down Viento Ridge as a counterclockwise loop becomes a bit vague where you must leave the continuation of the ridge N (ultra-difficult and bad option) at 2000 ft to head down the much more doable NW shoulder to the power line towers. Look out for ticks in spring and poison oak year-round. No fee. Restrooms with flush toilets present.

Large boulders stacked and partially embedded while leaning into the tree on the lower portion of Viento Ridge Trail.

TRAILHEAD: Starvation Creek State Park. *See* hike 30 for directions.

ROUTE: Walk past the restrooms toward Starvation Creek Falls to begin, and continue left easily on the paved HCRH State Trail that parallels the Interstate for a hundred yards to the semi-hidden TH for Viento Ridge on the right. It's 50 ft before and SW of a black metal gate (also see orange caution signs: "Keep Right" and "Rocks"). The faint path quickly becomes more pronounced ½ mi up about 26 moderately steep switchbacks by ferns, poison oak, a small cascade (off a short spur 13 switchbacks up), and only a few larger trees, climbing SSE to a clearing under a big power line.

Turn left at 900 ft in elevation at a semi-confusing juncture next to a tower, where climbing right directly back into the woods starts off flagged and leads even fewer Gorge scramblers on an alternate bushwhack route extremely steeply ESE up a shoulder to the main ridge as a slight shortcut. For this steeper WNW shoulder, climb to the right of the flag at the forest edge (above the first power line tower) on a steep traverse a few hundred yards far right (S) of the shoulder to

Strange lenticular clouds form near Mount Hood from Viento Point.

begin; then hike left back to the alternate WNW shoulder but still a few feet right (S) of it to avoid low flora up the super-steeps with little to no game trails in the middle section. The top section is more workable to the end (2200 ft at the bottom of the lowest brushy section blocking the main ridge crest, or almost 1 hour from the power line) without any solid paths that last, and will remain steeper than anything on the main NW shoulder and N ridge (of Viento Point) routes. A very tall still-standing dead pine at the bottom of a little clearing near the top is a landmark. Traverse left (NE) from the first power line tower above the switchbacks for the principal route instead through the clearing and hike a brief, steep brushy section on the trail, then continue around the cliffy area to the bottom of the NW shoulder route at the first of two more power line towers close together.

Say good-bye to most of the Gorge views for a while at more than a mile from the TH, as you turn right (SE) and head up the rocks steeply without much of a trail for a few feet to enter the thicker woods. See the flagging at the forest edge

Looking west at the bottom of Starvation Ridge, with Shellrock and Wind Mountains on opposite sides of the Columbia River.

perchance, and follow the strongest of many little paths just left (E) of the narrow ridge crest to the right of the flag; bushwhacking is the name of the game for the next 2½ mi to Mitchell Point Trail 417. The route is a bit foggy and marshy with faint paths crossing but best closer to the ridge from 1200 ft to 1400 ft and pretty obvious otherwise ½ mi to the main ridge. After scrambling past big moss-covered boulders lodged in the trees (1560 ft) and over many small branches covering the fairly steep path, the ridgeline turns more to the S at almost 2000 ft. Pick up the path again if you've misplaced it and begin to skirt the main ridge crest, with a more pleasant grade but about 30–50 ft or so to the right (W) around a few sets of brush and overgrowth that block easier travel along the ridgetop. As a hint you will leave the ridge crest at 2200 ft, 2480 ft, and 2800 ft if hiking uphill, and only for short stretches as the trail fades in and out.

At 3 mi from the TH, descend (for the first time) a small high point to a wide saddle with the ridge also widening (2900 ft) and many small downed trees partially blocking easier travel for the remainder (½ mi) that you can mostly avoid by staying on the path more to the right (SSW) off the actual ridgeline near the top, or continue straight up the ridge to a wide and flat ATV road (Mitchell Point Trail 417). The traverse path, like much of the main ridge, was well-marked with vertical sticks quite nicely by early summer 2015 until the path pitters out 75 ft directly under Mitchell Point Trail at FR-102. Bushwhack up briefly to Trail 417, turn right (SW) a few feet, take the first fork left (SE) on FR-102 (signed, starts wide) easily for ½ mi to Viento Point, and stay left into FR-104 ignoring any more forks to the end (with a great look down to Hood River) near FR-160. Turn left (S) a hundred yards on FR-160 to the point just below and S of the actual summit you just crossed over. The rocky, dirt-covered meadow breaks out of the woods with pleasing views of Mount Hood and Bull Run Lake below, as well as Mount Adams and Mount Defiance.

Avoid other ATV roads on the return for the shortest descent back to Mitchell Point Trail as FR-160 continues down S from the point and W from the juncture in the woods on a myriad of active ATV trails and loops, some brand-new but all a little confusing, and FR-1070 moves toward Mount Defiance and then SE from Viento Point. Turn left (SW) from FR-102 back onto Mitchell Point Trail for ¼ mi for the loop with Starvation Ridge to a wide saddle where it's slightly disorienting. USGS maps are a bit off, so *see* the map included here on p. 110. Follow the road ¼ mi to the end of the wide saddle, passing an ATV road on the left, and turn right at a 3-way intersection N toward the Gorge for ¼ mi to its apparent end (bushwhack only 50 ft farther W) or just before the end onto a thin path right 100 ft to Starvation Ridge Trail 414. Turn right (N) in either case opposite the trail and switchbacks left (SW) up toward Warren Lake.

Move down the steep path with a view of Mount Adams and the top of Mount Rainier, then work across the scree field on the left (W) side of the little gully on Trail 414 as you descend 8 switchbacks in the woods before traversing the last easier stretch NW without much pitch (relatively). At almost a mile from the start of Trail 414 at the wide saddle, hike S down the splendid slender ridge proper, where it is rocky and mellow briefly then quite steep on and off 2½ mi to the TH. *See* the beginning of hike 30 for a more detailed description of the lowest section and ridge, including 15 switchbacks under a power line, where you turn right at the Starvation Ridge Cutoff Trail 414B juncture below the switchbacks and then head right to finish along the Interstate (otherwise the trails are marked). You'll see dynamic views of Viento Ridge and the Columbia River from near the bottom of Starvation Ridge under the power line.

> **"The beauty of the natural world lies in the details."**
>
> **—NATALIE ANGIER**

ELEVATION: 1178 ft, with 1000-plus-ft vertical gain

DISTANCE: 1½ mi up including Mitchell Spur, more than 2½ mi round-trip for both

DURATION: 1½ hours up including Mitchell Spur, 2½–3 hours round-trip

DIFFICULTY: Moderate. Short but steep, clear trails. Some exposure near point, but it is not mandatory

Mitchell Point to Drano Lake and Cook Hill with a barge passing through the Columbia River on a calm day.

TRIP REPORT: The basalt outcrop rises more than 1000 ft from the Columbia River for two distinct points that give folks who don't have much time or may not be avid hikers a chance to stretch their legs and stand on top of a prominent landmark with incredible vistas. The nearby Wygant Peak Trail to the W from the same TH suffered hundreds of blowdowns with huge trees from ice storms early in 2012; it may not be passable for several years, if ever, although steps have been cut into a few trees to cross over. Frankly there are no views from the summit, and the vistas from below the top are okay but hardly worth the effort if you see the

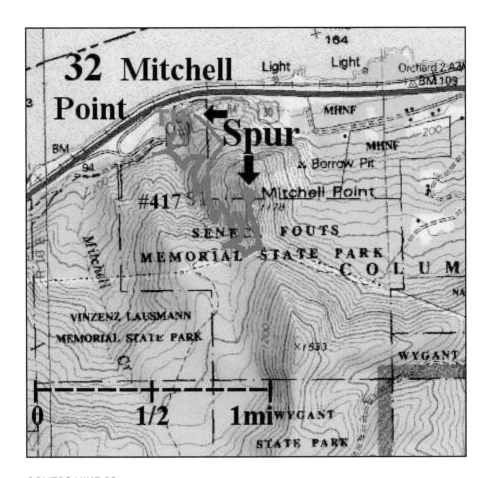

COVERS HIKE 32

mess. Use utmost caution if you feel the need to negotiate the old Chetwoot Trail or Wygant Peak Trail, mostly buried in big Douglas firs; it would be safer to leave it alone. No fee. An outhouse is present.

TRAILHEAD: Mitchell Point Overlook. From Portland, take I-84 E to exit 58 and the parking area at the end of the off-ramp. From the eastern Gorge, take I-84 W to exit 56 (Viento State Park), then drive 2 mi on I-84 E to exit 58. Return traffic westbound to Portland must drive a few miles E to exit 62 (Hood River) and proceed W on I-84.

ROUTE: Walk S from the large parking lot past the outhouse to the left on the paved trail as it changes to gravel. Stay left in a hundred yards on the very pleasant Mitchell Point Trail 417 as it meanders up 6 turns through the woods, watching for poison oak year-round. At about 550 ft in elevation and more than ¼ mi up, the main trail switches back to the right in the woods. Take a side visit or easier stroll from this switchback on the obvious path that continues about ¼ mi left (N) down, then up, a tad more steeply to Mitchell Spur, a high point lower on the ridge to Mitchell Point. This appears as a sharp triangular rock from the W and I-84 directly above the Interstate. The Spur provides a nicer overlook to the Gorge than from the parking lot without much effort. Just be cautious at the very top, especially with children.

Back to the main path, follow it for ½ mi, again much more steeply at times across the talus field, up more switchbacks, and through the lovely forest to a major saddle under a power line at 1000 ft. Hike left (N) almost ¼ mi to finish up the mostly treeless ridge littered with early season wildflowers and grand views of the Gorge, Mount Defiance, and mountains in Washington, including Dog Mountain to the W, Cook Hill above Drano Lake, the Little White Salmon River, and a trimmed shot of Mount Adams. Be careful: steep drop-offs on both sides dominate the area. Under ideal conditions only a few of the most experienced hikers investigate the last hundred feet of the point to the N on the razor-thin, bumpy ridge with substantial exposure from the high point and more popular viewing area.

33 | HOOD RIVER MOUNTAIN RIDGE

ELEVATION: 2100 ft, with 600–750 ft vertical gain

DISTANCE: 3 mi round-trip shortest loop; 4 mi round-trip short loop

DURATION: 2 hours round-trip shortest loop, 2½–3 hours round-trip short loop

DIFFICULTY: Easiest. Solid trail and road, simple hill climb, popular with locals

TRIP REPORT: April and May are best for wildflowers. Hood River Mountain's true summit (2495 ft) is unobtainable from the continuation of the ridge walk, as the trail passes through private property. In fact the entire hike is on a different private property owned by SDS Lumber Company, which has opened this land to the public (including mountain bikers) as long as people are respectful. The principal destination and what most people call the summit is simply a high point on the N end of Hood River Mountain's long ridge. Combine this hike with hike 34 to get more out of the day and drive. No fee or restroom.

TRAILHEAD: Take I-84 E to exit 64 (Hood River), turn right from the off-ramp more than ¼ mi to a stop sign, continue straight 2 mi on OR-35 S, turn left (E) on Whiskey Creek Drive ½ mi, turn left on East Side Road, then a quick right (E) up Old Dalles Drive 2 mi to the high saddle with parking on the right in front of the TH. Do not block the gate or driveway on the N side of the road.

ROUTE: Start S from the saddle past the "no motorized vehicles" sign up Hood River Mountain Trail. This is 100 ft W of the return loop on Old Dalles Drive, which turns right (S) after the saddle and eventually becomes Elder Road. Hike up the narrow trail through the thick woods gradually around a mile to the first viewpoints out of most of the trees. It can be windy from the lookout but loaded with wildflowers and expansive views of Hood River, the valley, the Columbia River, Mount Adams, Mount Hood, Mount Defiance, and others. The flat rocks at the apex make for a fitting picnic area. For counterclockwise loops, continue S along the open ridge more easily for a time, and turn left past the weather tower to stay on Hood River Mountain Trail, which now resembles a wide gravel road that leaves the ridge and meets Elder Road/Old Dalles Drive briefly. Turn left (N) for the shortest loop 1½ mi down the wider gravel road to your vehicle.

Wildflowers ablaze from a superior viewpoint on Hood River Mountain Ridge.

The slightly longer loop continues S along the ridgeline from the weather tower on the narrower trail, then through trees to a wide meadow, where you should walk left (E, then NE) on the solid trail to avoid private property. Return to the main road (Elder Road/Old Dalles Drive) where you finish left (N) very easily down to the TH. Or you could omit the loops and road walking to travel back the same route along the more tempting ridge trail.

> **"One touch of nature makes the whole world kin."**
>
> **—WILLIAM SHAKESPEARE**

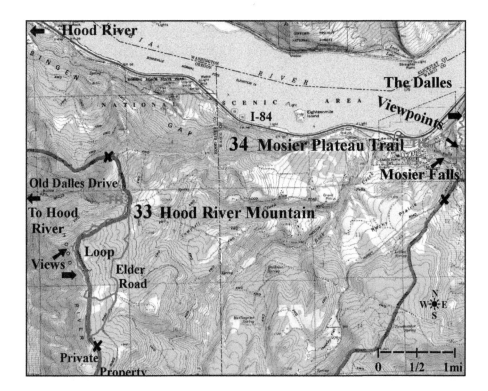

COVERS HIKES 33-34

34 | MOSIER PLATEAU TRAIL

ELEVATION: 580 ft at the high viewpoint, with 500 ft vertical gain, plus 350 ft to regain from the end of the plateau

DISTANCE: 1 mi to the high viewpoint, 2 mi round-trip; 1½ mi to the end of the plateau, 3 mi round-trip

DURATION: ½-¾ hour one way, 1½-2 hours round-trip to the end of the plateau and back, including Mosier Falls

DIFFICULTY: Moderate. Well-defined narrow trails, short walk and hill, switchbacks

---

TRIP REPORT: Friends of the Columbia Gorge volunteers finished the trail late in 2013 with help from Washington Trails Association and others. March through May is best for high flow on the falls, green grass, and wildflowers. Small snakes and ticks may be found close to the trail here. A few semi-hidden swimming holes for later in the summer are located between and below Mosier (Creek) Falls. Consider combining this hike with hike 33 or 35. No fee or restroom.

TRAILHEAD: Take I-84 E through the Gorge to exit 69 (Mosier), continue ½ mi across town on First Avenue (US-30 E), and park in the small pullouts where it is legal (and not signed otherwise) on either end of the bridge over Mosier Creek opposite the road at the bench signed for Mosier Pioneer Cemetery. This bench marks the beginning of the trail at the E end of the bridge. Or park in the center of town left after and E of the giant totem pole between the railroad tracks and US-30, and simply walk a hundred yards along US-30 to the bridge.

ROUTE: Climb the dirt path 30 ft above the bench to a better trail sign as it winds up through the grasses and wildflowers while overlooking the large canyon that leads into the Gorge. Pass a few headstones (Mosier family) and trees, then turn more to the left (SE) past the sign for Pocket Park into a much smaller canyon along Mosier Creek with a guard-railed viewpoint of the 70-ft (plus 10 ft above) cascading waterfall at less than ½ mi from the TH. A few experienced kayakers have even been known to run this creek on a good year.

Both tiers of Mosier Falls at dusk.

Continue E steeper as you traverse the very steep slope up 15 nicely graded switchbacks, including 3 sets of stairs on a few of them, and arrive at the high viewpoint with guardrails. There you will be greeted with a wonderful overlook of Mosier, the valley, and of course the Gorge. Walk N another ½ mi and 8 turns down the open plateau with small signs, deer, and wildflowers choking the path at times to the end. See tons of balsamroot, lupine, grass widows, and bachelor buttons among others in season. The brief loop near the edge of the plateau is fairly obvious and begins near a few trees as you see a bench on the left (W) fork of the loop. Full Gorge vistas unfold immediately, but especially of the unique, Coyote Wall, directly across the Columbia River. Finish the loop in either direction easily and return up passing near the communication tower, and then proceed down the same trail that ends at the bridge over Mosier Creek.

35 TOM McCALL POINT AND NATURE PRESERVE

ELEVATION: 1722 ft, with vertical gains of 1022 ft for Tom McCall Point, 300 ft descent to make up for down to Tom McCall Nature Preserve

DISTANCE: 1¾ mi up, 3½ mi round-trip; 1 mi down, 2¼ mi round-trip loop; almost 6 mi round-trip for both

DURATION: 1 hour up, 2 hours round-trip; 25 minutes down, 1 hour round-trip; 3 hours max round-trip for both

DIFFICULTY: Mix of moderate (for Tom McCall Point, narrow, steeper) and easiest (for Tom McCall Nature Preserve, many trails, wide-open, short-lived)

TRIP REPORT: March through June is best. The point itself is only open May 1 through October 31. No dogs are allowed, as this hike falls within the Nature Preserve. Wear pants: you may come across poison oak or even small rattlesnakes along the thin, sometimes overgrown trails. No fee or restroom.

TRAILHEAD: Rowena Crest Overlook. From Portland or Hood River, take I-84 E to exit 69 (Mosier), continue E on US-30 for 7 mi to Rowena Crest and the driveway to the parking circle on the right. From The Dalles, take I-84 W to exit 76 (Rowena) and follow US-30 W a few winding miles up to the driveway for Rowena Crest on the left.

Twisting road below Rowena Crest Overlook, with Tom McCall Point, Seven-mile Hill, and the eastern Gorge.

ROUTE: Find the trail on the left as you begin to walk out of the parking circle, and follow the old road S up next to the basalt-layered cliff rim, with the road zigzagging below and the eastern Gorge revealing itself in the same direction. After walking right at the Nature Conservancy's sign for McCall Point Trail, hike several switchbacks up a much steeper, narrower path S through trees with some open areas on or near the ridgeline, while keeping your goal in sight for most of the route. As far as rattlesnakes go, the young ones in the area might be the greatest hazard: they haven't grown their rattles yet and can't warn you when you get too close. That said, rattlesnakes tend to avoid humans, so you may only hear them slithering through the tall grasses, if at all.

Pass a multitude of wildflowers in season, especially on the windy summit plateau, as views W and E in the Gorge become dominant and you can see Mount

Balsamroot and lupine blowing in the wind from the summit plateau looking west down the Gorge.

Adams, Mount Defiance, and Mount Hood. There is a small saddle, another trail (rough bushwhack), and the ridge continuing up SE, but head down the way you came instead for the best egress. Then debate the Nature Preserve walk; it will be slightly anticlimactic compared to the point but has its own charm and is perfect for folks looking for a shorter walk on a pleasant plateau.

Begin Tom McCall Nature Preserve on the trail opposite (W of) the driveway and parking circle. Take the signed trail down right (N) past the posts and into the large meadow, staying left of any forks. Pass a surprisingly large pond surrounded by thick brush and trees on your right.

You can sneak closer views, though poison oak and bugs may deter you. Follow the path about ½ mi or so to the end, with several viewpoints down the cliff band to the Gorge and Lyle across the Columbia River. Return the same way or follow the slightly longer but more interesting loop trail along the cliff band just N of the main trail and catch the main trail again near the larger pond, as you walk either way around it to finish the last ½ mi back up to the road.

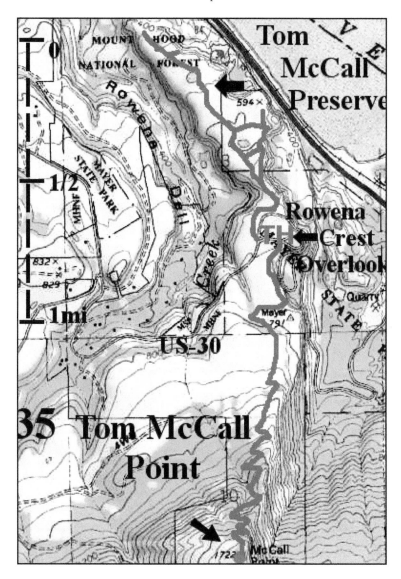

COVERS HIKE 35

ELEVATION: 1060 ft, with a 200 ft descent you must regain

DISTANCE: ¼ mi down, more than ½ mi round-trip around the park

DURATION: ¼ hour down, ½ hour round-trip plus time for pictures and lingering

DIFFICULTY: Mix of easiest (from the fenced viewing area, flat) and moderate (to base of the falls, steep, rocky, narrow paths, very short)

The best waterfall in the Tygh Valley near The Dalles.

TRIP REPORT: The Pacific Northwest never fails to entertain those willing to drive a couple hours or less to a completely different geological landscape, and these falls S of The Dalles in the Tygh Valley do not disappoint. The hosted White River Falls State Park is open for day use (no fee) roughly mid-March through October (check ahead), but spring runoff months hold the highest flow. No swimming as the undercurrents are too strong and dangerous. Restroom with flush toilets present.

TRAILHEAD: White River Falls State Park. Take I-84 E through the Columbia River Gorge to exit 87 (Dufur/Bend) at the E end of The Dalles, turn right ¼ mi, then left on US-197 S for 27 mi, and turn left on OR-216 E, following the signage 4 mi to the brief dirt road on the right.

ROUTE: Walk S from the parking lot on the dirt trails 200 ft easily to the closest viewpoints along a cliff band of the 100-ft-wide and largest tier of White River Falls. It's not much of a scramble per se, but to make the trip more worthwhile (and if the kids are eager hikers) you could visit the base of the surprisingly large 3-tiered waterfall (65 ft, 35 ft, and 5 ft high, in that order, top to bottom) by walking E over the visible wooden bridge with more steel fencing. Then turn right (S) and make your way carefully down the fairly steep little

All 3 tiers of the stunning White River Falls.

ridge over loose dirt and rocky paths. It becomes narrow as you make your way down to the right of the old power plant (worth checking out cautiously) and the ridge to the best view of all the tiers combined, although the highest falls become partly obscured. You can also work easier away from the edge down the wider path and steps to the left of the plant at the fork, and walk around it carefully. Step even closer by following the slim path left of the tiny cliff band to the rocks and better walking between the middle and lowest falls in the basalt-lined canyon. Return the same way.

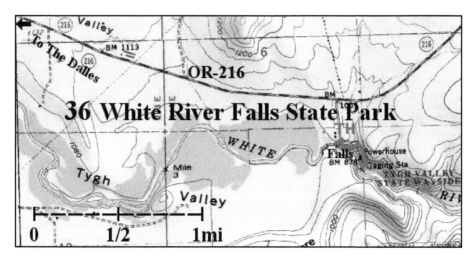

COVERS HIKE 36

ELEVATION: 1600 ft on Gordon Ridge, with 1400 ft vertical gain for the loop, otherwise mostly subtle ups and downs along the river corridor without much elevation change

DISTANCE: 5¼ mi one way to Gordon Ridge Camp on the Deschutes River, 10½ mi round-trip; 8 mi biking one way plus 8 mi round-trip loop hike (or not), 16 mi biking round-trip

DURATION: 2 hours one way, 4 hours round-trip; 5–6 hours bike-and-hike round-trip

DIFFICULTY: Mix of moderate (flat road to walk or ride, wide, thorny) and strenuous (for Gordon Ridge hike, bushwhacking, steep, long day)

TRIP REPORT: March through early May is best, when wildflowers are blooming and the canyon is bright green above the sizeable river. An occasional spring shower is much preferred to the midday searing desertlike heat of summer. With

very few trees, low flora, and a dry climate, this region is vastly different from the center of the Gorge. Look out for mountain bikers, ticks, and various snakes, all of which are plentiful in the canyon. If biking, use tubeless tires or a good tire sealant, and carry spares: thorns and sharper rocks are unavoidably plentiful. There are outhouses and camping spots throughout the canyon, but camping only comes with amenities at the TH. There is a $5 day-use or overnight fee from all parking areas.

Lower Deschutes River over spring lupine from Gordon Ridge.

TRAILHEAD: Drive 1½ hours from Portland on I-84 E through the Gorge to exit 97 (Deschutes River State Recreation Area), continue right 100 ft from the off-ramp, and turn left on OR-206 E for 3 mi to the campground on the right just past (E of) the Deschutes River Bridge. Stay on the paved road to the end of the narrow campground for the safest, hosted parking, or park in the day-use areas where there is space; otherwise hide the contents of your vehicle to help discourage break-ins.

Mostly level trail borders a cliff band for a short time adjacent to the Deschutes River.

ROUTE: Ride the pavement back to the start of the campground to the dirt road and Deschutes River Trail on the immediate right. If hiking, either head up one of the paths from the SE corner of the parking lot farthest S, or walk along the river path ¼ mi before it turns a few hundred feet SE up to the main trail. Walk or ride easily along the river 3¼ mi to Colorado Camp and 5¼ mi total to the smaller Gordon Ridge Camp. Then turn around to finish N back to the TH or continue ¼ mi S from Colorado Camp to the first railroad car, still fairly undamaged, and enjoy the enhanced views from within the canyon.

At the 8-mi marker there is an old trestle next to the trail, with the second railroad car just beyond. This is where the hike begins in earnest, up an old roadway known as the Rattlesnake Grade to the left leading up to Gordon Ridge. It is also possible to ride past the last camp and outhouses to the end of Deschutes River Trail 3¼ mi more (just past the old Harris Homestead and farm), but for now stash and lock your bike and begin walking up the trail (overgrown at first) opposite the trestle. Happily the road reveals itself soon enough, and you don't have to watch as much for snakes and can enjoy the increasingly improved views of the river valley. It's a steady 2½ mi up the Rattlesnake Grade to the end, where you turn left (W, then NW) 2½ mi along the Gordon Ridge plateau, immediately crossing the high point of the day to begin the traverse. You can see the trail and river valley below, with trains still running on the opposite side of the river and the rounded, treeless Gordon Butte rising to the right in the center of a large farming area on private property adjacent to the old jeep road. Mount Hood is closer, and the larger Mount Adams can also be seen on a clear day, with Haystack Butte (wind turbine–covered) directly across from the mouth of the Deschutes River.

Just SW of Gordon Butte, before passing by it, you arrive at a large power line tower and several confusing trails as the road ends. Leave the high ridge and plateau to hike left (W) directly after the power line tower down a fairly steep stretch more than ½ mi back to Deschutes River Trail. Follow the little gully down the paths on the left (S) side through small shrubs to the main trail, where you walk in the flats nearly 2½ mi back to the old trestle and your bike, initially passing the first railroad car again. Inspect your tires before the final 8 mi to the TH, where hopefully you have some cold, refreshing beverages awaiting in a cooler to help ease the pain!

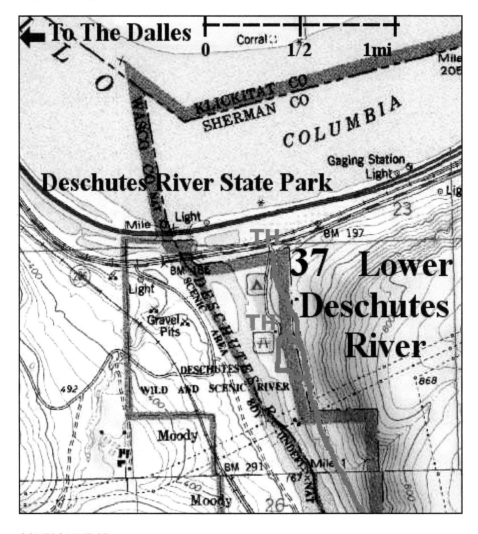

COVERS HIKE 37

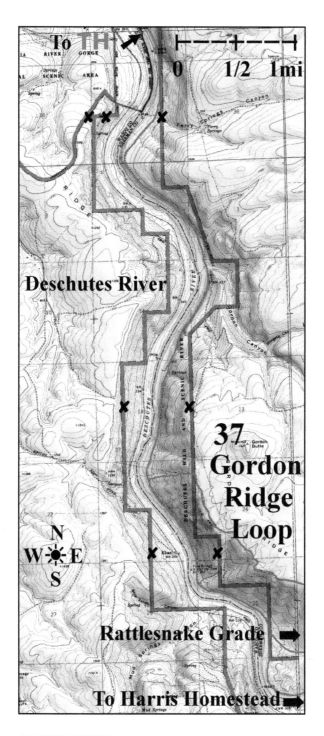

To TH

0   1/2   1mi

Deschutes River

37
Gordon
Ridge
Loop

N
W   E
S

Rattlesnake Grade →

To Harris Homestead →

COVERS HIKE 37

NGTON

(East to West)

WASHINGTON

38 | HAYSTACK BUTTE

ELEVATION: 2969 ft, with 869 ft vertical gain

DISTANCE: 1¾ mi up, 4 mi round-trip

DURATION: 1 hour up, 2 hours round-trip

DIFFICULTY: Easiest. Short gravel road walk, wide, quiet, not popular

Endless balsamroot in the early spring from Haystack Butte to Mount Adams.

TRIP REPORT: This hike is best in spring through mid-June before the grasses and wildflowers dry out. Combine it with hike 39 to get more exercise and rationalize the long drive if you're not coming from The Dalles or the Hood River area. No fee or restroom.

TRAILHEAD: Above Columbia Hills State Park. Take I-84 just E of The Dalles to exit 87 for US-197, turn left less than 3½ mi on US-197 N across the bridge into Washington, turn right on WA-14 E (Kennewick) 1 mi, turn left on Dalles Mountain Road 14 mi (mostly gravel, sometimes rougher, staying to the right at 3¼ mi near Dalles Mountain Ranch at the intersection for Stacker Butte). Continue straight (E) onto Rattlesnake Road after 2 mi of paved section and drive

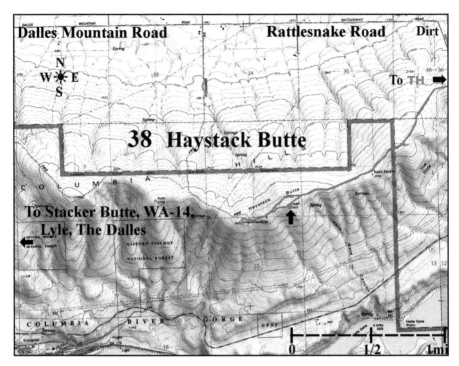

COVERS HIKE 38

directly toward the huge wind turbines more than 2 mi as it winds up the dirt and gravel road more steeply (S) to a saddle at 2114 ft. Park on the side of the road where it is safe, taking care to avoid blocking driveways or traffic. The gated service road (open to the public except "during construction activities") on the right is your TH. Alternately for less gravel roads or for Haystack Butte alone, take I-84 E to exit 104 (Yakima/Bend), turn left on US-97 N 3 mi into Washington, turn left on WA-14 W briefly, turn right on US-97 N 3½ mi to Spur Road on the left ¼ mi to Stringstreet Road, turn left 2 mi, and turn left on Dooley Road for 3¼ mi of roughly paved and gravel road steeply but okay for most 2WD to the top at a saddle and crossroads with the wind turbines maintenance road.

ROUTE: Start walking SW up the road along the treeless high ridge between the giant wind turbines that rule the landscape as far you can see looking E. At the halfway mark, leave the turbines to follow the

Walking amongst the giant wind turbines.

road and subsequent adjacent trail (watching for snakes) directly to the high point, which has minimal buildings compared to its sub-summit just to the W. Enjoy the views of the eastern plateaus of Washington and Oregon, the Columbia River, the Deschutes River (directly S across the Columbia River), and Mount Adams the other way to the NW. Walk to the sub-summit for a tiny loop without bushwhacking farther, and finish down the main road to the TH.

39 STACKER BUTTE

ELEVATION: 3220 ft, with 1150 ft vertical gain from the gated road at the official TH (plus 350 ft from the lower TH), plus 200 ft for Oak Spring Viewpoint spur

DISTANCE: 2½ mi directly to the summit only, 5 mi round-trip; 3¼ mi to the communication towers W of the true summit, 6½ mi round-trip; plus more than 1 mi round-trip from the lower TH or for Oak Spring Viewpoint spur

DURATION: 1½ hours up the standard route to the communication towers W of the true summit, 3 hours round-trip; plus an hour for Oak Spring Viewpoint spur

DIFFICULTY: Moderate. Dirt and gravel road walk, wide, steadily steep, switchbacks

Rain in the western Gorge but sunny in the east!

TRIP REPORT: Escape the rains and cooler weather that hang from the western Columbia River Gorge to Portland in April and May for a bluebird day with endless wildflowers. Watch for ticks, rattlesnakes, coyote, and deer to name a few. More developed trails within the adjoining Columbia Hills State Park, which runs from the parking for Stacker Butte down to Horsethief Butte (1¾ mi E of

A sea of gold from the road up to Columbia Hills Natural Area Preserve and Stacker Butte.

Dalles Mountain Road on WA-14) and lake, are closer to Horsethief Butte and worth inspecting further for short side trips or another outing altogether. Discover Pass required for all areas within the state park including parking for Stacker Butte. Restrooms are located at the campground, Horsethief Butte TH, and both ends of the lower trails, which go from Crawford Oaks TH (¾ mi E of Horsethief Butte TH) to the Dallas Mountain Ranch TH just E of the intersection for the Stacker Butte hike at a small sign to the left (N). Dogs are not allowed within the Columbia Hills Natural Area Preserve up to Stacker Butte, and all areas close at dusk except for the campground.

TRAILHEAD: Columbia Hills State Park. Take I-84 just E of The Dalles to exit 87 for US-197, turn left less than 3½ mi on US-197 N across the bridge into Washington, turn right on WA-14 (Kennewick) 1 mi to milepost 84½, and turn left on Dalles Mountain Road (gravel) 3¼ mi up to Dalles Mountain Ranch, where you fork left (N) at a small "339" marker then to more signage ("Dalles Mountain Ranch State Park Day-Use Only") and an open green gate. Drive almost 1½ mi more steeply, rougher and narrower but okay for 2WD to a gate and kiosk. Park in the minimal spaces without blocking the gate. It is also possible to park more easily ¾ mi up from the left-hand fork on a wider section of road off to the right next to a big green electrical box. This option will almost assure you a spot and give you more than ½ mi hiking each way along the beautiful wildflower-lined road.

ROUTE: Walk up the mostly treeless slope past the gate and by masses of balsamroot, lupine, Indian paintbrush, phlox, hotrock penstemon, Douglas' draba, and others. Head up the broad landscape on the old gravel road and 5 switchbacks a mile to a faint fork. The Oak Spring Viewpoint spur to the right past the rock pile on the fifth switchback heads E under the power line temporarily, then left (N) of a white sign and down a large old oak stand on the faded trail. Work past the uneventful and fenced-off Oak Spring less than ¼ mi farther to a break in the trees at an open viewpoint of Mount Adams and Mount Rainier on a clear day.

From the main trail continue up easier a short time past the first towers, then much steeper toward a fat rocket-shaped antenna on the summit. Meander left (W) more leisurely from the fenced-in antenna area along the high ridge, where there are a few taller communication towers to the end of the established road. Cruise around and gaze into the distance at most of the well-known big Cascade Volcanoes in two states. Swale Canyon begins NNE of Stacker Butte. You also have a grand view looking W down the Gorge, with Mount Defiance defining the highest point on the Oregon side. Return the same way, staying on the road while in the preserve.

Kaser Ridge in Oregon across a glassy section of the Columbia River near Horsethief Butte.

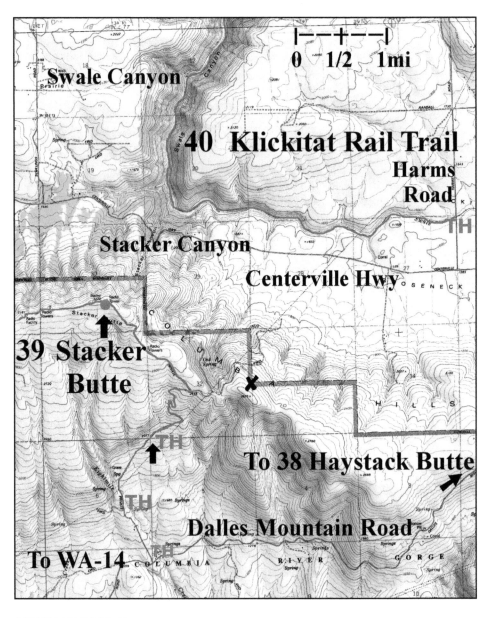

Swale Canyon

40 Klickitat Rail Trail

Harms
Road

TH

Stacker Canyon

Centerville Hwy

**39 Stacker
Butte**

TH

To 38 Haystack Butte

Dalles Mountain Road

To WA-14

COVERS HIKES 39-40

ELEVATION: 1530 ft at the top of Swale Canyon, with 1000 ft vertical gain from the bottom

DISTANCE: Up to 13 mi one way walking or biking Swale Canyon, 26 mi round-trip (same trail); 11 mi mountain biking Horseshoe-Bend Road to finish with a loop, 24 mi round-trip

DURATION: Up to 4–5 hours one way walking the entire length, 8–9 hours round-trip; 6–7 hours round-trip hike-and-bike in Swale Canyon, or round-trip loop with more difficult hike-and-bike

DIFFICULTY: Mix of moderate (easy grade walking or biking up one way, or down a few miles and back up to the top of Swale Canyon, wide) and strenuous (bottom to top, very long, desert climate, tiring mountain bike loop, steep finish)

TRIP REPORT: Walk or bike the entire route or travel as far as you wish and return up or down Swale Canyon. Many people park at the top of the canyon and hike or bike down to begin, as the views are admittedly better the top half of the canyon, but then you must return uphill to finish, which is always slightly more awkward. Your choice. The old railroad grade was converted into a long, sometimes rougher gravel trail, and the 13-mi stretch covering the length of Swale Canyon is very gradual, gaining only 1000 ft over the span—a far cry from the average 1000 ft per mile in the center of the Gorge!

A desert feel, including a lack of big Douglas firs, gives this hike a vibe different from others between Hood River and Washougal. Early spring months are best. Keep a watchful eye out for deer and meadowlarks, as well as rattlesnakes and ticks. The trail is closed July through September because of heat and fire danger but is otherwise open in spite of any signs to the contrary. Stay on the main trail and keep dogs on a leash due to the adjoining private property near the bottom (where squatters have been living free for decades). No fees. Portable outhouses are located at both THs.

TRAILHEAD: Take I-84 E to exit 64 (Hood River), turn left on OR-35 N (White Salmon), pay the $1 toll to cross the Hood River Bridge into Washington, turn right on WA-14 E 11 mi to Lyle, turn left on Lyle-Centerville Highway 14¾ mi, and turn left on Harms Road ½ mi to the upper TH and sign at the top of Swale Canyon. Lock a bike near the bridge for the return ride to the lower TH later, either down Klickitat Rail Trail or along the gravel road to finish. To drive to the

One of several bridges over the creek on the Klickitat Rail Trail.

lower TH (Wahkiacus) at the bottom of the canyon, continue N on Harms Road 2 mi, turn right on Niva Road a few feet, turn left (N) 5 mi on Harms Road again as it becomes Horseshoe-Bend Road, turn left (W, still Horseshoe-Bend) 4 mi, winding much more steeply and more bumpy down to the lower TH. The lower TH is E of the bridge over Klickitat River on Horseshoe-Bend Road and to the right 50 ft down Schilling Road on the right. To begin directly from the lower TH, or to leave a shuttle vehicle there to hike the trail one way, turn left on WA-142 E for 16 paved mi from WA-14 in Lyle to Klickitat Rail Trail at Wahkiacus, turning right on Horseshoe-Bend Road briefly and right on nearby Schilling Road for 50 ft.

ROUTE: Bring the family and walk (best choice for most) or ride (more difficult with children or as a loop) as far as you wish from either TH over several well-built bridges (except for one that is easily bypassed) and trestles along Swale Creek with a few tiny waterfalls, tons of wildflowers, and a broadening green canyon near the top. Pass by a few structures, old cars, and trailers the bottom 4 mi or so. Then the journey becomes prettier as you meander effortlessly up the top half of Swale Canyon. Stacker Canyon and Stacker Butte come into view near the last turn to the left (E). You will have a more expansive landscape and sky near the uppermost part of the canyon and creek. Cross the water one more time over the highest footbridge near the Harms Road TH.

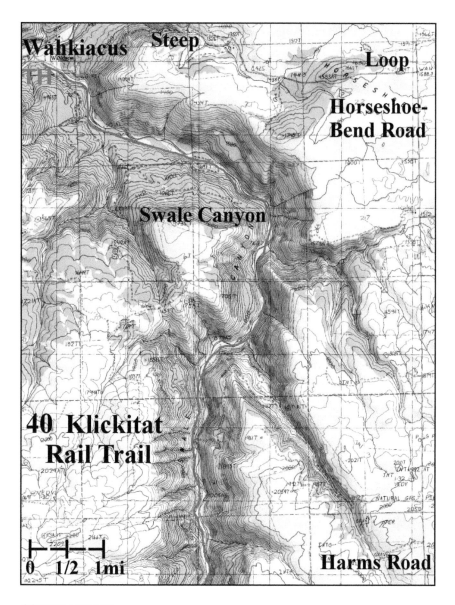

Wahkiacus TH
Steep
Loop
Horseshoe-Bend Road
Swale Canyon
40 Klickitat Rail Trail
Harms Road

0 1/2 1mi

COVERS HIKE 40

"Look deep into nature, and then you will understand everything better."

—ALBERT EINSTEIN

ELEVATION: 620 ft; 870 ft; with vertical gains of 360 ft for the shortest loop, 610 ft for the 3-mi loop

DISTANCE: 2 or 3 mi round-trip loops; or 1 mi alternate paved universal loop without the arch

DURATION: 1–1½ hours round-trip all loops

DIFFICULTY: Mix of easiest (less than ½ mi directly to the arch or separate brief universal access trail [Catherine Creek Trail 4400]) and moderate (short loops, narrow)

TRIP REPORT: Look out for poison oak and small snakes. No fee. A portable outhouse is present February through early May—also the best time for wildflowers and the season for rain farther W in the Gorge near Portland and Vancouver. Dogs must be on a leash. There is also a 1-mi paved universal access loop trail that is fairly flat and provides close-up views of the Columbia River and of petite Catherine Creek Falls.

TRAILHEAD: Take I-84 E to exit 64 (Hood River), turn left on OR-35 N (White Salmon), pay the $1 toll to cross the Hood River Bridge into Washington, turn

right on WA-14 E (through Bingen) almost 6 mi, and turn left before (W of) Rowland Lake on paved Lyle White Salmon Road (Old Hwy 8, milepost 71) 1½ mi to parking spaces on the left. Less than 70 mi and 70 minutes from Portland or Vancouver.

Lupine dominates near Catherine Creek.

ROUTE: To stroll directly to the arch, walk right (NE) at the immediate fork (opposite the closed FR-015 trail) and up the signed wide trail FR-020 as it turns into FR-021 at the next fork to the right. Cross the creek immediately over the little bridge and head into the woods to a meadow less than ½ mi from the TH. You will see a wooden fence and an old corral opposite Catherine Creek Arch, which lies in the middle of a large basalt rock wall. It is hard to see the sky through the arch and difficult to photograph. Please do not cross the log pole wooden fencing indicating the closed area around the arch. Return the same way or easily reverse the description below for a clockwise loop.

File photo of Catherine Creek Arch.

To hike the loop in a counterclockwise direction finishing with the arch, walk less than ¼ mi E from the TH along the paved road, cross Catherine Creek, and look for the thin path up the hill to the left (N) after the guardrails. Follow it through the wide-open meadows on a steady grade that varies only minimally in steepness over the solid and sometimes rock-embedded trail, passing endless wildflowers with nice views of the Gorge and Mount Hood 1 mi to the next junction. After ½ mi from the paved road, contour above the rock wall and arch beside more log pole fencing not to be crossed.

Wind up and see a large power line crossing a little bump on the ridge and a break in the long wall with a bailout trail you may take a hundred yards left (W) to begin the descent. As a few pines and other trees begin to appear, you can see the trail confluence in a meadow where you can cruise left again (S) down the main trail on FR-021 less than ½ mi more steeply to the next meadow, the corral, and Catherine Creek Arch (left). Finish less than ½ mi across the creek into FR-020 (gravel) as the terrain opens up again and you are able to spot your car parked along Lyle White Salmon Road. Easily extend the walk another mile by continuing up the hillside past the power line and bump on the ridge for almost ½ mi. Turn left at a few cairns that direct you back into the tree-filled gully heading S toward the Gorge less than ½ mi to the confluence

Stunning bitterroot flower.

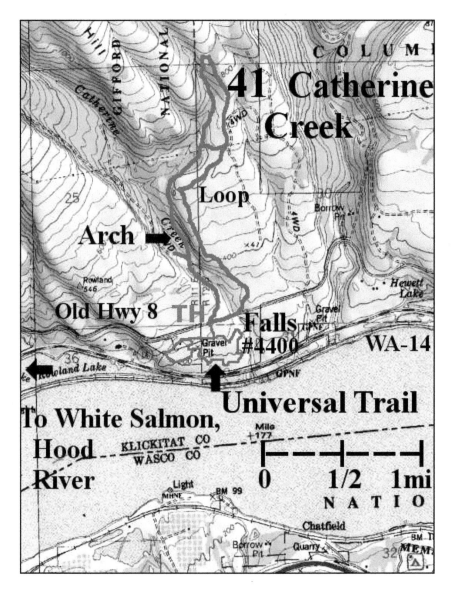

COVERS HIKE 41

under the power line with a USFS sign that reads "hiker only—dogs on leash all year." Finish as described above.

    The universal trail is completely paved and wheelchair-accessible. Start S of the main TH across the old highway and turn left at the first fork to view Catherine Creek Falls (25 ft high) and an old oak stand in less than ¼ mi. There are a couple of brief loop options, the longest being more than a mile total through the open field with temporary ponds, wildflowers, a stiff breeze, and good views of the Gorge along the way. *See* the map above for the loops.

42   COYOTE WALL LOOP

ELEVATION: 1630 ft at the top of the meadow adjacent the wall or cliff band; 1220 ft at the top of Labyrinth Loop; 1750 ft at the top of Atwood Road Loop; 2180 ft near the top of Burdoin Mountain; with vertical gains of 1530 ft directly, 1120 ft for Labyrinth Loop, 1650 ft for Atwood Road Loop; 2080 ft for the longest loop, utilizing Bristol Road at the top briefly

DISTANCE: 2½ mi up one way, 5 mi round-trip; 6 mi round-trip Labyrinth Loop (plus ½ mi round-trip for Lower Labyrinth Falls spur); 6¾ mi round-trip Atwood Road Loop; 10½ mi round-trip Bristol Road Loop

DURATION: 1–1½ hours up one way, 2 hours round-trip no loop; 2–3 hours round-trip Labyrinth Loop; 4–5 hours round-trip longer counterclockwise loops

DIFFICULTY: Mix of moderate (nice grade straight up Coyote Wall, steady, several semi-confusing paths, brief steeps in the Labyrinth, no signs with trail names well into 2015 but fairly obvious) and strenuous (for the longest loop, gravel road walking, steeper)

TRIP REPORT: The Forest Service closed private property W of Coyote Wall until suitable trail placement can be worked out around Burdoin Mountain; the system will eventually connect more clearly (watch for signage) with the Catherine Creek area. Respect the closure, as there are plenty of emerging options E of Coyote Wall, which is a long, 200-ft-high cliff band made of columnar basalt formed long ago during the Missoula Floods. The cliff curves up with a large, sloping meadow and small canyons with smaller volcanic outcrops that reside just E, perfect for outdoor escapades, and the landmark can easily be seen from across the Columbia River in Oregon. Look out for bikers and equestrians, as well as ticks, poison oak, and birds of prey. April, May, and sometimes June are truly inviting when it's still raining in Portland and before it gets too hot and the wildflowers and grasses dry out. Bring the dog and kids and prepare for a windy, dry climate. No fee, and an outhouse is present.

Smaller and quaint but pleasant, Lower Labyrinth Falls.

TRAILHEAD: Take I-84 E to exit 64 (Hood River), turn left on OR-35 N (White Salmon), pay the $1 toll to cross the Hood River Bridge into Washington, turn right on WA-14 (Lewis and Clark Highway) E 4½ mi (milepost 69½), turn left on Courtney Road, and park immediately in the designated little parking area on the right.

ROUTE: Walk E past the wooden posts at the beginning on the old highway ½ mi around Locke Lake, past big boulders and rocks scattered across the road from Coyote Wall above—you will realize why they moved the highway! Around the corner is the end of the counterclockwise loops or direct route up Coyote Wall Trail between a couple wooden fence boxes on the left. For that, simply head up the main trail and hike left (NW) at any junctures where biking trails fork right. Stay closer to the western edge of the cliff band as a rule of thumb, being careful near the lip (especially if it's windy) while getting that perfect picture. It's a bit steeper the first ½ mi or so, and the views of Mount Hood, Mount Defiance, and the Gorge unfold right away as wildflowers begin to mix in. Hike about 1½ mi more, with the views outward and of Coyote Wall and the flowers becoming grander, up to the top of the big meadow at a nondescript area near tree line. Have a picnic near the huge and mossy old downed evergreens and return the same way for the easiest but certainly not the most stimulating of the many routes. *See* the map on p. 148 and try a loop from the clues below.

Trails that continue W down from the top of the wall onto private property should be avoided. Trails to the E and N of Coyote Wall pass through public spaces

Looking up the sheer basalt of Coyote Wall near dusk.

Lush green rolling hills in the spring dominate the eastern Gorge from Coyote Wall Trail.

but come close to private property. Please be respectful, pack out all trash as always, and keep off closed trails, which evolve and change based on many factors, including the need to revegetate areas eroded by mountain bikers.

Counterclockwise loops from the old highway may be preferred, as you would come down Coyote Wall Trail to finish when the lighting is better against the cliff band later in the day. At ¾ mi from the TH, Labyrinth Trail (also called Hidden Canyon Trail) begins at the Forest Service sign on the left (N), but you should take a detour first, not even ¼ mi farther along the old highway to the often overlooked Lower Labyrinth Falls. There is one little cascade en route to the Labyrinth area, then the fanned-out, nearly 25-ft-high falls coming down the mossy rock next to the trail, with several picture-perfect angles toward the Columbia River. Visit this waterfall and Labyrinth Falls before they nearly dry up in summer.

Back to Labyrinth Trail for all counterclockwise loops, begin N as there is a fork upcoming to the left for Little Maui Trail and falls. Stay right up the main and most worn trail through a notch less than ½ mi to first see Labyrinth Falls through the thin trees. A couple paths move to the nearby creek for a better shot of the 30-ft (or so) narrow cascade. Two quick switchbacks up the steeper trail takes you directly above the falls to what could be called Upper Labyrinth Falls, another 30-ft thin cascade, but this one with a more suitable backdrop. You've got the Gorge of course and the columnar basalt cliffs above the little canyon with a ton of color everywhere in season.

Cross the wooden plank over the creek on the easygoing trail, continuing N above the falls area through scree and oaks. At about 1½ mi from the old highway in the open meadow along the traverse, turn more steeply left (NNW) up the ridge near a single huge pine tree on the same path (Hidden Canyon Trail), which meanders in and out of old oaks past tons of poison oak ½ mi to the next juncture (Atwood Road/Trail). Stay left (W) more than ¼ mi down, up, and down toward Coyote Wall on the wide trail, and see Mount Hood if you haven't yet for some reason. Cross the creek over the little footbridge, and walk up briefly to a major intersection at the edge of the forest. This is the high point of Labyrinth Loop at 3¼ mi counterclockwise from the TH.

Ignore all trails that head right, instead working out to the far left to the mostly open meadow again for the shortest return down the old jeep trail SSW 1¼ mi to Coyote Wall Trail and others passing a couple of small creeks that dry up en route. From Coyote Wall Trail, stay to the right (W) at the junctures near the cliff band for the most direct pedestrian trail a mile down to the old highway, with wide-open vistas the entire way. The biker trails between the Labyrinth and Coyote Wall areas are slightly to mostly rutted (thanks to poor planning, even though some restoration has been helpful), have their own names, and zigzag over more ground. Directly below the old jeep trail is a traverse path E to the 2 steeper bike routes, the first being Little Moab closer to Coyote Wall on the continuation right (S) after a turn, with the left choice at the upcoming fork moving E then S down Little Maui Trail (somewhat more amusingly following the creek and another falls area near the bottom, where the remainder is visible more to the right toward the old highway).

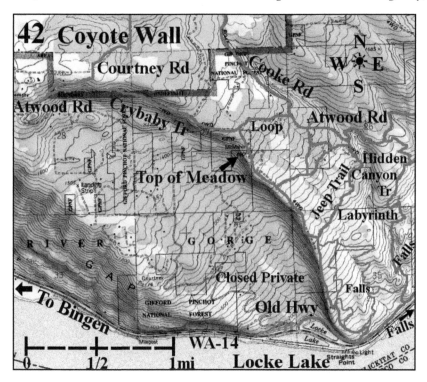

COVERS HIKE 42

For longer loops from the intersection at the top of Labyrinth Loop, head right NNW to stay on Atwood Road ¼ mi as it narrows past a metal gate to another juncture. The slightly longer option to this meets at the same juncture and has two more shorter possible loop alternatives to the top of Coyote Wall, unless the trails on public lands that pass by adjoining private property are closed. (Look for no-trespassing signs or closed gates.) Follow a narrower path that lies 10 ft left of the Atwood Road intersection at the top of Labyrinth Loop and heads right (W) up a short section through a rise in the woods to a gravel road near Burns Farm. Going left moves by the private property ½ mi to Coyote Wall. In a moment you will encounter another option if you need to bail left (SW) to Coyote Wall (between double wooden posts on each side of the road) for ½ mi, walking down to meet the other path, then right across a small creek and up to Coyote Wall Trail just below the highest meadow viewpoint and turnaround.

Less than ½ mi total from the top of Labyrinth Loop on the widening path, arrive at the juncture with Atwood Road (main route past metal gate at the middle fork) and stay left for ¼ mi to a white gate at the next crossroads. This is about 3 mi from the start of Labyrinth Trail at the old highway. Left is Atwood Road moving W straight past what appears to be someone's yard but is really the trail on public lands. Turn left easily finding the route for the preferred loop and traverse ½ mi to Coyote Wall. Walk 30 ft past the wide fork left in the woods to the next one left (S) at a sign and down Crybaby Trail for better views. Pass the old trail (closed) moving down to the right and arrive at the nearby highest meadow turnaround on Coyote Wall near the big old fallen pines. For the longest loop option from Atwood Road at Cooke Road, turn right steadily up the wide road past another sign, this one correctly stating "primitive rd no warning signs next 1½ mi." At the end turn left (W) on FR-1310/Bristol Road less than ½ mi down to Courtney Road. See Mount Adams to the N through part of the clear-cut section along the way.

Turn left (S) on Courtney Road around 1¼ mi as it curves around to Atwood Road. Turn left, walking past a dead-end sign, "primitive road next 1 mile" sign, and "private property, stay on trail" signs. The road narrows past big Douglas firs and becomes the wonderful Crybaby Trail through the woods on a traverse above and N of Coyote Wall to a partially signed junction. Instead of continuing E on Atwood Road/Trail, turn right down the solid path briefly to the top of the meadow, where most people hiking up will stop next to Coyote Wall. The next juncture while heading down moves left ¼ mi over a creek and then up steeply at the fork left or right (E) ¼ mi down and up to Atwood Road/Trail by Burns Farm (wooden posts, *see* above) near the top of Labyrinth Loop for an alternate loop to the Labyrinth area (watching for closed or private signs). Or just hike directly down to the TH about 2 mi, following the cliff band to the old highway, then right ½ mi to the parking area. And *see* above for biking and hiking loop options directly below the old jeep trail in the Labyrinth.

ELEVATION: 200 ft or so, descending more than 500 ft from Cook-Underwood Road, then back up to return

DISTANCE: ¾ mi one way, 1½ mi round-trip

DURATION: ½ hour one way, 2 hours round-trip with quality time spent at different viewpoints

DIFFICULTY: Strenuous. Positively steep, very brief, fairly solid trail, scree, drop-offs, potentially muddy or icy path. Use traction devices in winter. Not family- or pet-safe

---

TRIP REPORT: One of the most magnificent yet undervisited falls in the Gorge (or anywhere for that matter) is on the Little White Salmon River in Washington. The chief reason fewer people make their way to it is the super-steep path. The main falls drop only 33 ft or so but are about 75 ft wide. Only the most badass kayakers run the Class V river and huck all of the falls in the area during a non-spectator race held annually in late May. Please avoid the inevitability of being

Thunderous luminescent curtain of Spirit Falls!

Translucent turquoise waters down only about 6 feet at Chaos Falls and relatively easy for kayakers still in their boats, but extremely dangerous if they end up swimming for it and drop on the near side to the right.

turned away without proper, preapproved credentials: come another time, as overcrowded trails will damage sensitive areas rapidly and will be fairly dangerous to hike next to cliffy sections surrounding the waterfalls. January through mid-May is best for winter or high-flow scenes on the colorful river. Look out for poison oak. No fee or restroom.

TRAILHEAD: From Portland, take I-84 E to exit 44 (Cascade Locks), turn right up the circle to cross into Washington over Bridge of the Gods ($1 toll required), turn right on WA-14 E 14 mi (9 mi past the first exit for Carson, and past Wind and Dog Mountains), turn left just W of Drano Lake (milepost 56½) on Cook-Underwood Road for 2 mi, and come to a large parking area in the dirt on the right side of a sharp corner from the paved road.

ROUTE: With no trail signs, it's a little confusing from the start, and the short hike will be tougher if the trail is wet, frozen, or snow-covered. There is a worthy view of the river and fish hatchery from the S corner of the parking area. For the principal route, begin at the hidden TH between the "milepost 2" and "35 mph" signs to the right (E) down through the woods. You will parallel but must avoid private property and a private road that lie just left (N) the entire way to the falls.

Follow the scree and moss-covered rock path very steeply ½ mi SE, zigzagging straight down the semi-clearing to more trees. Stay on the most worn path (cairns and flagging probable) a bit more easily down to the river, finishing slightly left steeply again to a tree-covered ledge in the woods above the lower falls known as Chaos. These falls are impressive in their own right, as is the entire river corridor!

Work your way up the well-defined trail a couple hundred yards left (N) around to the top of the upper falls, where you can actually peer down right next to the most powerful plummet, thanks in part to a huge tree clinging on near the lip. Be mindful of others and of the trail here, which sits right next to steep drop-offs into the bright blue river. While there is not exposure on the trail itself, a slip or fall into the river could certainly be fatal. The path continues through the woods more easily above the largest drop for a few feet to a calm and safer area to soak your feet or have a picnic. The breeze on the riverbank vacillates strangely between very cool and very warm on the same day. Enjoy the the rainbow effect and feel of the falls from several semi-precarious angles, and return the same way 15–20 minutes up the steep hillside.

> **"In all things of nature there is something of the marvelous."**
>
> **—ARISTOTLE**

44 | DOG MOUNTAIN LOOP

ELEVATION: 2930 ft (summit is 2948 ft), with 2800 ft vertical gain

DISTANCE: 3 mi up Dog Mountain Trail directly, 6 mi round-trip; 4¼ mi up from Augspurger (Mountain) Trail, 8½ mi round-trip; around 7¼ mi round-trip loop connecting both trails

DURATION: 1½ hours up Dog Mountain Trail directly, 2½ hours round-trip; 1¾ hours up from Augspurger Trail, 4 hours round-trip; 3–4 hours round-trip loop

DIFFICULTY: Mix of moderate (for Augspurger Trail, steady, wide, longer) and strenuous (for Dog Mountain Trail, many steep and narrow switchbacks, very popular)

Classic shot from Dog Mountain in May looking west over Wind Mountain to the Columbia River.

TRIP REPORT: This loop is well liked year-round as a shorter Gorge hike, providing ample exercise and superb views, but is most frequently visited in May and early June when balsamroot and other wildflowers blanket the mountain. It might even be tough to find a parking spot in the ginormous lot on weekends. Parking along the highway is illegal. By all means, hike up and down directly or save your knees and take the loop in either direction. Both routes described here will travel one way to the top. A Northwest Forest Pass or fee is required. There is a vault toilet at the E end of the parking lot 200 ft up the trail on a switchback.

TRAILHEAD: Dog Mountain TH. From Portland, take I-84 E to exit 44 (Cascade Locks), turn right up the circle to cross into Washington over Bridge of the Gods ($1 toll required), turn right on WA-14 E, and go 12 mi, past Wind Mountain, to a very large parking area on the left at milepost 53. From Vancouver, take WA-14 E to the same locale. Dog Mountain Trail 147 is far to the right at the E end of the lot.

ROUTE: For the fairly steep ascent, begin on well-traveled Dog Mountain Trail 147 more than ½ mi up 11 switchbacks to a signed juncture. Climb right (NE) on the main trail for a total of 20 steep switchbacks from the bottom to the top, with views getting progressively better, especially from the Lower Viewpoint (1600 ft) and then Puppy Dog Lookout site (2505 ft) to the highest meadow through the thinning trees. You will have scrumptious Gorge vistas, including that of nearby Wind Mountain, the mountains of Oregon (including Mount Defiance), and truncated looks at Mount Hood and Mount St. Helens on a clear day. The "more difficult" trail option from the signed juncture more than ½ mi up from the TH is just that, with sparser views and fewer people; it is a bit shorter, taking you to meet Trail 147 again at about 2000 ft. Another less frequently utilized option is just above Puppy Dog Lookout from the main trail and steep meadow heading right (NE, then NW) at a juncture. This optional trail is longer and moves into the woods until near the very top. It eschews the windy, open slopes with wildflowers and better views and may be taken to avoid worse weather or being run over by the masses on weekends in the spring.

At the high intersection with Augspurger Trail 4407 (which contours down to the NW), turn right at the sign and finish with a couple more switchbacks less than ¼ mi to the general end. Most people stop at the highest golden meadow before the trees and actual summit, but on a clear day Mount Adams can be seen through an opening from the path that continues just into the trees. Come back to the meadow as the summit path soon pitters out and splits up in the thick brush and fallen trees. One barely discernible trail leads to an uninviting, overgrown, and difficult-to-access high point worth skipping. Return the same way, or indulge in a loop down Trail 4407 by easily following the signage and reversing the description below.

Augspurger (Mountain) Trail begins up left (W) from the right side of the large parking lot. It is slightly longer to meet Dog Mountain Trail than the sign indicates, about 4 mi. Head more N up the trail as lupine and paintbrush begin to appear alongside thick flora and ferns in spring and early summer. See Grant Lake below and Wind Mountain not far to the W. After nearly 3 mi of gradual walking, with only 2 switchbacks, turn hard right at a signed crossroads and continue more than ½ mi along a steeper, narrower stretch SSE up the ridge with 2 more switchbacks. Contour almost ½ mi around the W face and steep, wildflower-covered slopes of Dog Mountain to the brief summit trail on the left at the intersection with Dog Mountain Trail. Finish the final steep switchbacks to the turnaround meadow near the peak. Have a picnic and finish with a clockwise loop in half as much time down the escalator ride that is Dog Mountain Trail.

"Earth laughs in flowers."

—RALPH WALDO EMERSON

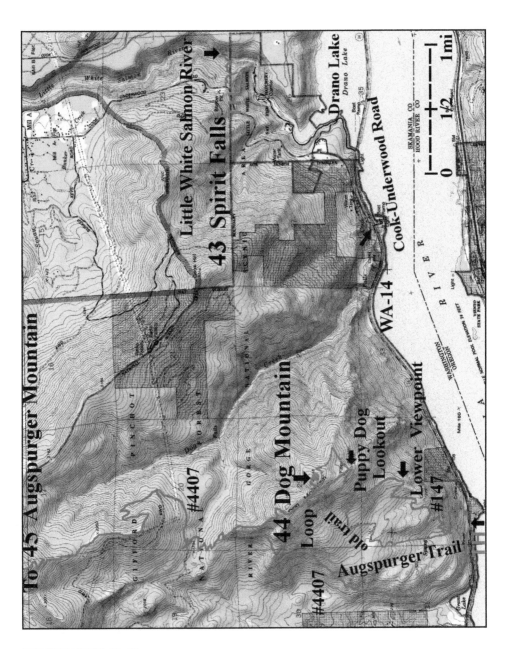

COVERS HIKES 43-45

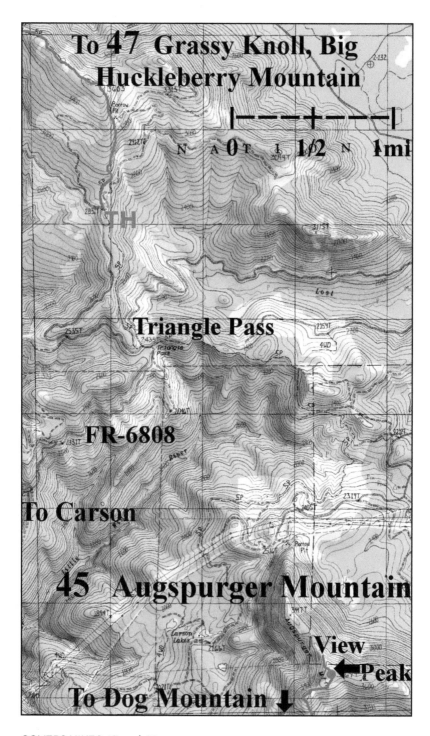

To 47 Grassy Knoll, Big Huckleberry Mountain

Triangle Pass

FR-6808

To Carson

45 Augspurger Mountain

View Peak

To Dog Mountain

COVERS HIKES 45 and 47

ELEVATION: 3667 ft, with 4100 ft vertical gain total including the viewpoint N of the peak

DISTANCE: 7½ mi one way, 15 mi round-trip

DURATION: 3 hours one way, 6 hours round-trip

DIFFICULTY: Very challenging. Steep ups and downs, confusing logging roads, narrow, rather long

---

TRIP REPORT: Best in late May through June for enjoying wildflowers before the trail becomes overgrown and is more problematic to follow. Dog Mountain can be tacked on at the end to make a difficult, lonesome hike even more difficult but less lonesome! Keep your eyes open, as wildlife encounters could include a black bear or even (rarely) a mountain lion. A Northwest Forest Pass or fee is required. There is a vault toilet at the E end of the parking lot 200 ft up the trail on a switchback.

TRAILHEAD: Dog Mountain TH. *See* hike 44 for directions.

ROUTE: Augspurger (Mountain) Trail 4407 begins up left (W) at the sign on the right side of the large parking lot. Head more to the N up the wide trail, which in spring is lined with wildflowers. After nearly 3 mi of gradual walking up the slope, including a couple of switchbacks, reach a ridgeline junction and sign where Dog Mountain Trail turns right (S) and Augspurger Trail continues left (N) a mile down the ridge, losing 430 ft (you will have to regain later) on the thin, steep path to the valley below. Stay on track through the thick and large trees to the very bottom, as the trail thankfully turns into a wide old road. Follow the road right (E, then NW) more easily around ½ mi, winding up to a clearing under power lines with many options. Ignore them all to stay on the

Grand Lake and the river from Augspurger Trail.

main trail and old road directly across (NE), and head back into the woods to the next intersection. This will be on a corner where the road heads left and you continue straight (N) to stay in the woods on the distinct trail, winding around the ridgetop more easily for a bit and through clearings. You will have views of Wind Mountain, Dog Mountain, and others, as well as Mount Defiance in front of Mount Hood across the river.

Cascade Volcanoes from the viewpoint beyond the summit of Augspurger Mountain.

The route will be steeper and apparent another mile up, staying fairly close to the ridge through the scattered trees to a little high point just SW of Augspurger Mountain, where you have a solid look at the tree-covered viewless summit ¼ mi away. Enjoy some easier walking along the wide ridge section on the thinning path to the unexciting peak in the thick woods. Do not dismay, however, as your efforts will soon be rewarded. Continue left (NNW) on the obvious trail down a different little ridge (past reflectors nailed to trees, indicating the top area) only 5 minutes and 100 ft loss in elevation to about 3560 ft. There at the top of the clearing you will have first-rate views of the Gorge and three big Cascade Volcanoes—well worth the brief jaunt after coming so far. The path extends about ½ mi to a little bump on the same ridge to the NW, if you need to prove a point. Otherwise return by the same trail or add Dog Mountain for a slightly longer route with a much steeper yet quicker descent.

> **"One sees great things from the valley; only small things from the peak."**
>
> **—G. K. CHESTERTON**

ELEVATION: 1907 ft, with 1000 ft vertical gain

DISTANCE: 1½ mi up, 3 mi round-trip

DURATION: 1 hour up, 1½–2 hours round-trip

DIFFICULTY: Moderate. Steadily steep, wide, switchbacks, short-lived

The Columbia Gorge lures many with its subtle beauty in winter.

TRIP REPORT: No fee or restroom.

TRAILHEAD: From Portland, take I-84 E to exit 44 (Cascade Locks), turn right up the circle to cross into Washington over Bridge of the Gods ($1 toll required), turn right on WA-14 E 7½ mi to milepost 51, turn left on Wind Mountain Road 1½ mi, turn right on Girl Scout Road ¼ mi as the paved road turns to gravel at a little pass, and park on the side.

ROUTE: Continue SE down the gravel road less than ¼ mi to the unmarked but discernible trail on the right heading up SE. Watch for poison oak encroaching the solid trail ½ mi to the little spur path, which takes you very steeply and briefly left (N) to an okay overlook. Check out the viewpoint (or not) and climb the sometimes rocky trail another mile and 8 switchbacks total to the top with even

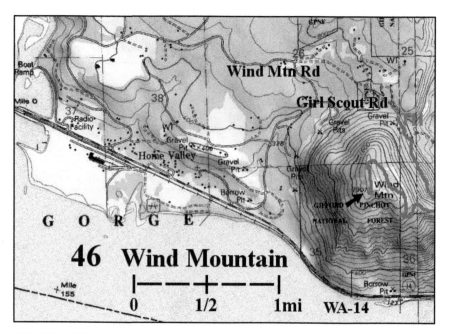

COVERS HIKE 46

better vistas, especially of Dog Mountain, Mount Defiance, and Wind Mountain's cousin, Shellrock Mountain, directly across the Columbia River. Return the same way, staying on designated trails at all times.

Nearby snowcapped Dog Mountain from Wind Mountain.

ELEVATION: 4202 ft, with close to 3000 ft vertical gain with ups and downs

DISTANCE: 5½ mi one way, 11 mi round-trip

DURATION: 2 hours one way, 4–5 hours round-trip

DIFFICULTY: Mix of moderate (steady uphill to Grassy Knoll, fairly short) and strenuous (to Big Huckleberry Mountain, long, easier ups and downs, narrow)

TRIP REPORT: With a fun 2-hour drive to the TH from Portland, abundant wildflowers in May and especially June, outstanding views for much of the walk, and very few people around, this is one of the best gems still close enough to be called a Gorge hike! It's also enjoyable in the fall when the huckleberries ripen and the summit lives up to its namesake. Various wildlife may be encountered along the way, such as black bear, mountain lion, black-tailed deer, coyote, bobcat, or elk. No fee or restroom.

TRAILHEAD: Near Triangle Pass. From Portland, take I-84 E to exit 44 (Cascade Locks), turn right up the circle to cross into Washington over Bridge of the Gods ($1 toll required), turn right on WA-14 E 5¾ mi, turn left (N through

Mount Adams and Little Huckleberry Mountain across Big Lava Bed.

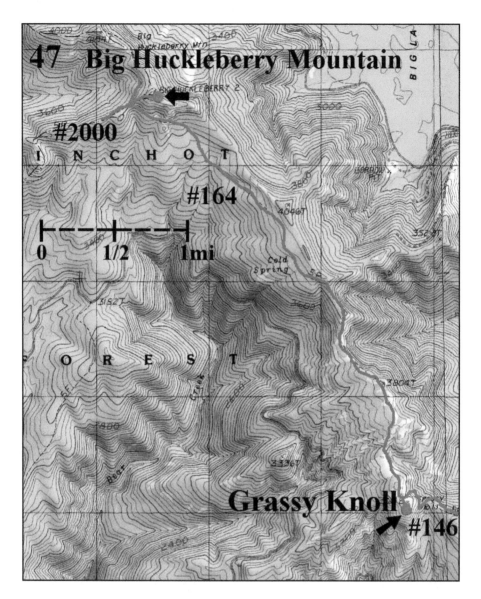

COVERS HIKE 47

Carson) on Wind River Road 4 mi, and turn right on Bear Creek Road (FR-6808) 3½ mi. The paved road turns into gravel and narrows on FR-6808 for 7¼ mi to Triangle Pass. Stay left on FR-68 for 2 mi up to the parking lot on the right at the juncture with FR-511. From Vancouver, take WA-14 E to the same locale.

ROUTE: Begin N up the meadow past the sign for Grassy Knoll Trail 146 and head into the woods a mile to the first good views, this one NE to Mount Adams behind Little Huckleberry Mountain (across Big Lava Bed). Work your way over

Grassy Knoll from the less-traveled trail en route to Big Huckleberry Mountain.

the crest of the ridge and see Grassy Knoll to the NW, as the approach is a bit steeper to the wide flat summit (3648 ft) on the well-defined trail. Mount Hood is visible and only gets better. Call it a day at 4 mi round-trip or not.

After the first 2 mi to Grassy Knoll, including the short spur path left to the wide top (and lookout foundation remnants) and back, continue NW along the ridgeline or just left (W) by wildflowers up and down 3 mi more to an intersection with the PCT in the thick woods. It's never too steep as you climb to the right from the sign E for $1/2$ mi to the wide-open, grass-covered summit with lovely views of Mount Hood, Mount Adams, and the Columbia River. Return the same way.

Indian paintbrush light up a steep meadow to Big Huckleberry Mountain.

48 GREENLEAF PEAK

ELEVATION: 3422 ft, with 1920 ft vertical gain

DISTANCE: 2 mi up, 4 mi round-trip

DURATION: 1 hour up, 2 hours round-trip

DIFFICULTY: Strenuous. Some steeps, logging roads, narrow to peak, drop-offs

---

TRIP REPORT: This short hike is fun year-round, with decent elevation, some views, and no one around. Deep snow is possible during a "normal" winter. No fee or restroom. Drive cautiously: logging trucks rule the back roads. Check skamania.com/columbia-river-gorge for more adventures in the area.

TRAILHEAD: From Portland, take I-84 E to exit 44 (Cascade Locks), turn right up the circle to cross into Washington over Bridge of the Gods ($1 toll required), turn right on WA-14 E 1½ mi and just past milepost 43, turn left on Rock Creek Road (toward Skamania Lodge), take the second left onto Foster Creek Road ½ mi as it turns into Ryan-Allen Road another ½ mi, turn left on Red Bluff Road ¾ mi, and turn left on FR-2020 for 3 mi on a semi-rough road (not bad for most with 2WD). Park safely on the side of the road where it is possible as you arrive at the fifth power line crossing. The hike begins as a 4WD road following the power line for a bit. From Vancouver, take WA-14 E to the same locale.

Mount Adams from Greenleaf Peak in winter above the clouds.

ROUTE: Begin the hike SW up the steep, unsigned 4WD road in the clearing, as the route begins to switchback several times pleasantly 1½ mi to a saddle with many options. Turn left (ESE) ½ mi to the peak from the saddle as the path becomes narrower and much steeper to the tiny top, where you have limited views because of the trees but nice shots of Mount Adams, Mount St. Helens, and Table Mountain. Return the same way. For those who wish, a rough path continues very steeply down the ESE ridge through the trees more than ¼ mi and almost 500 ft (you will have to regain) to a limited view above the huge cliff band below known as the Red Bluffs (seen clearly from Oregon and I-84, not unlike the sheer cliffs of nearby Table and Hamilton Mountains). This will change a relatively simple hike into a much more strenuous one with bushwhacking. Pay attention near the precipice.

49 | TABLE MOUNTAIN LOOP

ELEVATION: 3417 ft, with 3367 ft vertical gain

DISTANCE: 4 mi up, 8½ mi round-trip counterclockwise loop

DURATION: 2½ hours up, 4½ hours round-trip counterclockwise loop

DIFFICULTY: Very challenging. Positively steep at times, narrow, scree, drop-offs, well traveled

TRIP REPORT: Although it is nearly impossible to attain the summit in deep winter, this prominent landmark is quite delightful most other times, with huge vertical cliff walls similar to its neighbors. Restroom present. Day-use fee is $5 to park, payable at the Bonneville Hot Springs Resort and Spa desk. Feel free to check out the Lounge for snacks or cocktails after the hike, or book a room in advance if you are visiting the region (bonnevilleresort.com).

TRAILHEAD: Dick Thomas TH (*see* hike 50 for the alternate, unestablished Aldrich Butte TH). From Portland, take I-84 E to exit 44 (Cascade Locks), turn right up the circle to cross into Washington over Bridge of the Gods ($1 toll required), turn left on WA-14 W 3 mi to milepost 38½, turn right (N) under the railroad bridge on Hot Springs Way, turn right immediately on Cascade Drive nearly ¾ mi, turn right onto E Cascade Drive into Bonneville Hot Springs Resort and Spa, and drive slowly and respectfully left (W) of the hotel to the large gravel parking area. From Vancouver, take WA-14 E 3½ mi past Beacon Rock, then left on Hot Springs Way to the same locale.

From the perilous perch on Table Mountain to one of the most expansive looks of the Gorge!

ROUTE: Walk W up the gravel road a couple hundred yards as it curves right to a juncture. From here turn left 20 ft and cross the wider road to the thin, overgrown (at first) Dick Thomas Trail on the right for a mile NW to the end, traversing easily up through the beautiful forest. Cross the creek at the Carpenters Lake outlet over the little log footbridge and see Table Mountain across the meadow. At the nearby juncture, turn right (N) 60 ft, then left (W) almost 200 ft up steeper turns and away from the narrow trail that runs next to the dry lakebed known as the Two Chiefs Trail or Greenleaf Falls Trail. Turn right (N) at the next intersection, as opposed to the wide old road heading left (S) less than a mile steeply to Aldrich Butte. Continue a mile a bit more steeply up the Cedar Creek drainage as the PCT parallels the wider road (Table Mountain Trail), then meets it as you take either route N another 250 ft, then the PCT to the right (still N) ½ mi without difficulty to the next junction and beginning of the loop. West Ridge Trail moves N toward the summit straightforwardly but also quite steeply in ½ mi if you wish to avoid the ultra-steeps or take the loop in a clockwise direction.

To bang out the hardest part of the day first on the counterclockwise loop, climb right (N) like a little mountain goat by the signage for Heartbreak Ridge Trail, and up the super-steep narrow path more than ½ mi before you begin to have decent views. Traverse left (W) ¼ mi somewhat more easily after the sweat fest, but then you must ascend the huge scree field up the clearing very steeply more than ¼ mi and about 500 ft N, following cairns and posts marking the route through the boulders to the top, where you escape to the left on the more solid trail. It's actually more fun than it looks, but take your time in case you find some unstable rocks.

Hike right at the last forks to walk more easily less than ½ mi E to an exciting viewpoint overlooking the Gorge, Greenleaf Peak, and a few big Cascade Mountains. Be mindful of huge drop-offs down the cliff band and while checking out a small semi-hidden seasonal waterfall over the edge to the W. Notice several lakes below of different sizes to the SE, including Kidney and Gillette Lakes, with Wauna and Ashes Lakes being the largest and closest to the Columbia River.

Have a picnic where it's safe to do so. Then walk W along the flats of the mesa and summit area less than ½ mi, soaking in the vistas before turning left at the trees and heading steeply down West Ridge Trail a mile S, with fewer views, to the end at the PCT. Turn left (E) ½ mi on the PCT and traverse to the end of the loop with Heartbreak Ridge Trail. Resume down to the Dick Thomas TH, recalling that last left turn (E) at the Carpenters Lake meadow, and don't follow the wider old road S toward the Aldrich Butte TH (unless you parked there or wish to complete a longer loop back to the resort). *See* hike 50 for the longer loop, the hike to Table Mountain from the smaller Aldrich Butte TH, and for loops around Aldrich Butte into Cedar Creek.

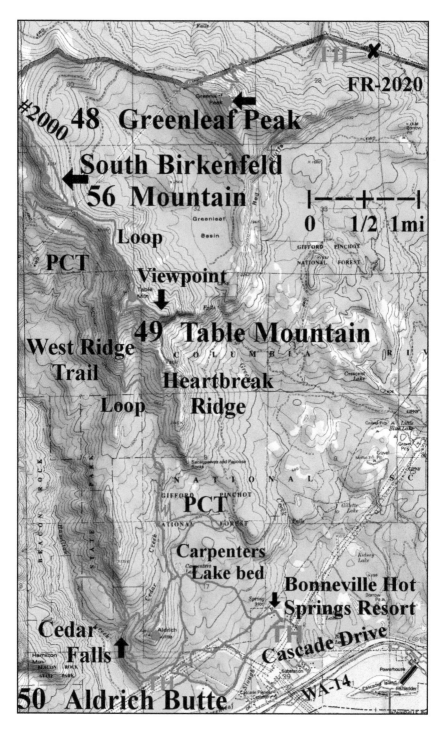

FR-2020

#2000

48 Greenleaf Peak

South Birkenfeld
56 Mountain

0   1/2   1mi

Loop

PCT

Viewpoint

49 Table Mountain

West Ridge
Trail

Heartbreak

Loop   **Ridge**

PCT

Carpenters
Lake bed

Bonneville Hot
Springs Resort

Cedar
Falls

Cascade Drive

50 Aldrich Butte

WA-14

COVERS HIKES 48-50 and 56

50 ALDRICH BUTTE TO CEDAR FALLS LOOP

ELEVATION: 1141 ft, with vertical gains of 1100 ft for the summit alone, around 1400 ft including loops into Cedar Creek

DISTANCE: 2¼ mi up, 4½ mi round-trip; 4½–6 mi round-trip loops

DURATION: 1 hour up, 2 hours round-trip; 3–4 hours round-trip loops

DIFFICULTY: Moderate. Some steeps, becomes wider, better than expected views, possible loops with lack of signage, Cedar Falls Spur not ideal for families

TRIP REPORT: This hike can be combined with hike 49 for a much more difficult trek, but it deserves its own listing for folks who just don't want to work that hard or who wish to tack on a slightly more difficult side visit to the intriguing Cedar Falls area. Restroom present only at Dick Thomas TH, where there is a day-use fee of $5 to park, payable at the Bonneville Hot Springs Resort and Spa desk. There is no fee at the much smaller Aldrich Butte TH. Wildlife encounters are possible, including deer and elk.

TRAILHEAD: Dick Thomas TH. *See* hike 49 for directions or use the nearby unestablished Aldrich Butte TH. For that, continue 1 mi past Bonneville Hot Springs Resort and Spa on Cascade Drive as it becomes gravel over the narrow Carpenter Creek Bridge into Shelly Lane a hundred yards to a fork. Turn right onto the rougher maintenance road, where there are a couple of easier parking spots in the pullout on the left, and just a few more spots another hundred yards or so up the steeper road section to 2 nearly immediate 3-way junctures. Park sensibly between the junctures, under the power lines, without blocking any of the roads.

ROUTE: *See* below for routes beginning from Aldrich Butte TH. From Dick Thomas TH, walk W up the gravel road a couple hundred yards. As it curves right to a juncture, turn left 20 ft and cross the road to the thin, overgrown (at first) Dick Thomas Trail on the right for a mile NW to the end, traversing easily up through the beautiful forest. At the juncture, turn right (N) 60 ft, then left (W) almost 200 ft up steeper turns and away from the narrow trail that runs next to Carpenters Lake (dry).

Turn left (S) at the next intersection and continue up the wide old road (Aldrich Butte Trail) fairly steeply less than a mile to the summit, where you'll see a few stone stairs and part of the base left from an old lookout tower. Even though the area is mostly overgrown, there are still full shots of Bonneville Dam, the Gorge, Beacon Rock, the mountains of Oregon, Table Mountain, South Birkenfeld, and nearby mostly tree-covered Cedar Mountain. If you are not into the side trip and possible loop into Cedar Creek, return by the same route, remembering to walk E by the Carpenters Lake meadow on the final mile or so to your vehicle at the resort.

The fairly concealed Cedar Falls is tucked below Aldrich Butte to the W. You can get to it via a rougher trail that takes off to the left from Aldrich Butte Trail more than ¼ mi down from the summit and descends less than a mile directly to the base of the falls on steep narrow paths that can only be reached when dry. If coming up Aldrich Butte Trail, fork to the right (SW) at a little saddle on the high ridge more than ¼ mi above the intersection with the Table Mountain Trail. Take the traverse down on Aldrich Cutoff Trail, which thankfully is privately maintained yet unsigned for ¼ mi, then more steeply down 2 quick switchbacks to a juncture. Hiking left takes you on a pretty easy loop around Aldrich Butte to both THs and is described below. Head right on Cedar Creek Trail by the big cedars, cottonwoods, and Douglas firs about 100 ft down to cross Cedar Creek wherever possible. It will be more difficult during times of high water, but that mossy tree 30 ft up the stream or others may be negotiable.

Elusive Cedar Falls down the steep drainage.

Continue up a couple hundred yards and begin to see the top tiers of the falls down to the left, the main one through the trees and directly above the longest drop of Cedar Falls being 10 ft high. Look up to the right immediately from a little shoulder for a faint path that heads up to Cedar Mountain, but stay on the main path briefly to another shoulder and second path and very steep bushwhack up to nearby Cedar Mountain. Turn left instead at this quiet 4-way intersection and hike the thin but solid path quite steeply, winding down to the mossy rock- and tree-lined creek at the base of the long cascade (80–100 ft total) less than ½ mi from the creek crossing above.

Return the same way up steeply or add an additional mile or so for a little loop within the loop option. This follows the slightly overgrown path down from the falls and creek bed briefly and easily, then moves NW up to the right of

Hamilton Creek. Head right (ESE) at the halfway mark, away from the creek, and up through the trees with some (mostly limited) views, and proceed around the alcove more easily up to the quiet 4-way intersection. Continue on Cedar Creek Trail and cross the creek again to the juncture, where you either turn left (NE) steeply to the Aldrich Butte Trail or continue right (S) on Aldrich Cutoff Trail for the loop around the butte 2–3 mi more to Dick Thomas TH, or 1 mi more to Aldrich Butte TH. Keep in mind that most of the loop route is on private property but is open to the public as long as the trails remain pristine. A few more loop options will arise if the resort is your goal, but none are too difficult.

Walk ½ mi from the juncture to the falls near Cedar Creek as you contour S up and then down under Aldrich Butte, with views of Hamilton Mountain and Cedar Mountain mostly through the trees, and finish down steeper turns to the end near another faint junction. Turn left onto a wider trail more than ¼ mi in and out of the woods and under big power lines. Notice truncated Beacon Rock behind you to the SW. When Aldrich Cutoff Trail ends, turning left will take you N up the old Aldrich Butte Road steadily and pleasurably less than a mile to Carpenters Lake, where you turn right more than a mile down to Dick Thomas TH for the longest loop option.

Turn right on old Aldrich Butte Road and proceed around a bend to the next nearby option under the power lines at Aldrich Butte TH. You could follow the rougher maintenance road left (NE) more than a mile with minor ups and downs and then stay left away from the power lines finally back into the woods. You would turn right at the last little juncture down a couple hundred yards around the corner to the parking area at the resort.

Staying right under the power lines on old Aldrich Butte Road (into Shelley Lane turning left) is the easiest loop option and is only slightly longer as the dirt road becomes level and paved, becoming Cascade Drive after the Carpenter Creek bridge. Follow the water along the Greenleaf Slough for a mile, then turn left into the resort to find your vehicle on the left.

For routes from the Aldrich Butte TH, walk up old Aldrich Butte Road steeply between large underbrush 500 ft to the forest edge and the first of several crossroads to Table Mountain, Aldrich Butte, or the Cedar Creek area, all of which are unsigned until near the Heartbreak Ridge Trail on Table Mountain. Meander pleasantly straight up the wider Aldrich Butte Road less than a mile N to Carpenters Lake for direct routes to Aldrich Butte or Table Mountain. Or hike left (SW) from the juncture at the forest edge on the narrowing Aldrich Cutoff Trail, then more steeply on Cedar Creek Trail, as the drainage is lush with ferns, Oregon grape, and pines for only around 1½ mi directly to Cedar Falls.

ELEVATION: 2438 ft, with 2038 ft vertical gain from the official TH (2200 ft from Beacon Rock TH on WA-14)

DISTANCE: 3½ mi up Hamilton Mountain Trail, 8 mi round-trip including spurs for the counterclockwise loop from the official TH

DURATION: 1½–2 hours up, 2½–4 hours round-trip loop or not

DIFFICULTY: Strenuous. Steep, more than 50 switchbacks, narrow, drop-offs, clearly marked trails

---

TRIP REPORT: This hike packs a wallop into less vertical gain than many high points in the area and is popular year-round when more lofty destinations are buried in snow and ice. When the road to the official TH and a campground is gated and closed in winter, simply begin from the bottom at the parking for Beacon Rock and walk almost ½ mi up to the official TH. A Discovery Pass or $10 fee is required for both, and restrooms are located at both THs. Beacon Rock is the

Rodney Falls from the bridge in autumn.

Dramatic landscape from Hamilton Mountain Trail.

easiest place in the Gorge to receive a pricey ticket for noncompliance. Also note that the gate is closed and locked to vehicular traffic every day at dusk. Remember this if you are camping or getting a late start.

TRAILHEAD: Beacon Rock State Park. From Portland, take I-84 E to I-205 N into Washington to the first right for WA-14 E (exit 27 toward Camas) for 27 mi, or take I-5 N into Washington to the first right for WA-14 E (exit 1A) for 34 mi. From Vancouver, take WA-14 E 34 mi to milepost 35, park on the right side of the highway on either side of Beacon Rock, which is evident suddenly, or turn left (N) to the official TH opposite Beacon Rock and drive up the paved road (with a small green "campground" sign and gate) almost ½ mi to the sizeable day-use area on the right before the campground.

ROUTE: Start in the woods from the official TH past the outhouse and signage NE to a clearing under a power line, where the trail on the left from the campground meets within the first ½ mi. See the summit of Hamilton Mountain unobstructed from the trail and benches near the juncture. Continue NNE ½ mi more to a decent, fenced-in view of Hardy Falls (90 ft high) a few feet down the spur path on the right, with Upper Hardy Falls far above the bridge from the main trail. The more interesting Rodney Falls (80 ft high, 2-tiered) with Pool of the Winds are almost ¼ mi farther, including up the short spur trail on the left. Spring months are best for the full effect near Pool of the Winds. Remember to water-proof your camera before another fenced-in viewing area.

Hike NE up more steeply from the falls area (2 switchbacks on both sides of the creek) for ½ mi to the Hardy Creek Trail and return route for the counterclock-wise loop on the left. Climb the steeper route right instead with big firs, ferns, and low flora. A massive cliff band begins to define the ridge with a few enticing views outward for almost another 2 mi to the summit. You'll work up nearly 20 switch-backs, enjoy a short break near the ridge crest (making you think you are close), and then ascend over 30 more tight switchbacks to the summit! Panoramas from the very top can be semi-obscured near the post, but with all the high brush there is still an excellent shot of Table Mountain to Birkenfeld Mountain to the NE, and sometimes you can make out part of Cedar Falls below Aldrich Butte. The current summit post reads 2488 ft; off a bit from what's listed here (official USGS), and GPS consistently shows even less but what can you do? The bushwhack path S down through the scrub brush may not be worth it. Two long ribbons of water fall side-by-side after good rains from the sheer cliff facing Oregon.

You can return the same way, but vistas of the Gorge, Hamilton Mountain, Mount Hood, Mount Adams, Aldrich Butte, Beacon Rock, and Table Mountain vastly improve if you follow the narrow ridge trail N for ¾ mi, including down a couple of switchbacks and then along a wider, rocky section to a major saddle. Only a couple hundred yards N of the summit lies a short path to the right up a small bump on the ridge, which offers a better look at Cedar Falls and a nice semi-private picnic spot.

For the counterclockwise loop back to the TH, follow the signage left (W) off the ridge from the flat saddle intersection and down a rocky old road to begin, but leave the remainder of the steeper, wide road at the first nearby switchback. There you will find more pleasant walking (trails meet below) right (NW) into the woods down Don's Cutoff Trail for almost ¾ mi, including a few switchbacks near the bottom. The only Don that can take credit for this one is Don Cannard, who cofounded Chinook Trail Association and did a lot of early trail work in the Gorge. Keep left (S) when the alternate path ends at the wide Hardy Creek Trail for 1½ mi of leisurely walking to the end of the loop above Rodney Falls. Pass an outhouse on the right, then the more tedious rocky road route on the left within the first ½ mi. Continue down the wildflower-surrounded main trail, staying E of the creek at another crossroads to the Hamilton Mountain Trail juncture, where you turn right past the falls area 1½ mi to the TH.

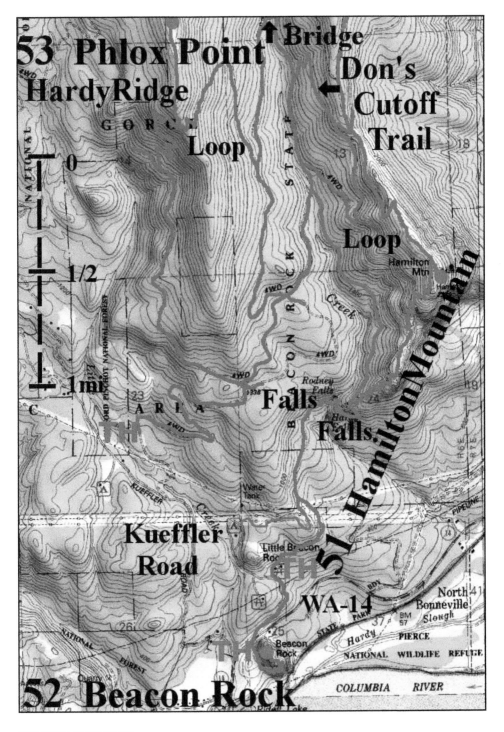

53 Phlox Point

Hardy Ridge

Bridge

Don's Cutoff Trail

Loop

Loop

51 Hamilton Mountain

Falls

Falls

Kueffler Road

WA-14

52 Beacon Rock

COLUMBIA RIVER

COVERS HIKES 51-53

ELEVATION: 848 ft, with 750 ft vertical gain

DISTANCE: 1 mi up, 2 mi round-trip

DURATION: ¼–½ hour up, 1 hour round-trip

DIFFICULTY: Moderate. Brief but steep, drop-offs, slippery when wet, guardrails

Beacon Rock late in the day casts a formidable shadow.

TRIP REPORT: Sorry, that's Beacon Rock, not Bacon Rock—don't get any ideas! Columbia River Gorge visitors have used the extra-large monolith as a landmark for hundreds of years. It was in fact named by Lewis and Clark in 1805 during their famous trek to the Pacific Ocean. Technical climbing is permitted at times on the S wall, but an astonishingly well built trail exists beginning on the W side, with several bridges and walkways that crisscross each other up dozens of switchbacks with incredible views all the way to the summit. It's relatively safe, but keep young children close for the short walk, and avoid bringing dogs. The trail is closed and off-limits by means of a big door near the bottom at the beginning of the more hazardous area from dusk until 8 am every day. A Discover Pass or $10 fee is required (only TH where a credit card is acceptable payment), and this is the easiest place in the Gorge to receive a pricey ticket for noncompliance. Restroom present.

TRAILHEAD: Beacon Rock State Park. From Portland, take I-84 E to I-205 N

Wauneka Point (tree-, rock-, and snow-covered bump on the high ridge) and McCord Creek across the Gorge from the crazy path up Beacon Rock.

into Washington to the first right for WA-14 E (exit 27 toward Camas) for 27 mi, or take I-5 N into Washington to the first right for WA-14 E (exit 1A) for 34 mi. From Vancouver, take WA-14 E 34 mi to milepost 35 and park on the right side of the highway on either side of Beacon Rock, which is quite recognizable.

ROUTE: Follow the signed route S pretty easily through the woods for a moment, with the enormous boulder towering above to the left. Informative signs along the way and on top tell about the geology and recent history. Walk through the doorway and stay on the only trail up all the switchbacks on the semi-tree-covered monolith to the summit, as you applaud the engineering creativity and dangerous work it took to build such a route. See much of the Gorge from the apex, including nearby Hamilton Mountain and Bonneville Dam.

ELEVATION: 2957 ft, with 2200 ft vertical gain

DISTANCE: 4½ mi up, 9¼ mi round-trip loop including summit

DURATION: 2 hours up, 4–5 hours round-trip loop including summit

DIFFICULTY: Mix of moderate (loop without summit, steady with some steeps, equestrian roads, signed) and strenuous (Phlox Point, drop-offs, longer, rocky)

TRIP REPORT: This underrated loop in Beacon Rock State Park has plenty of charm, extensive views from a wide-open ridge, and is easygoing enough for the whole family to complete even if you omit the last stretch up to Phlox Point. Visits are possible year-round with snowshoes, although it may be windy and cold in winter. Late spring through summer is the best time for wildflowers. A Discover Pass or fee is required, and a restroom is present and open year-round.

TRAILHEAD: Beacon Rock State Park. From Portland, take I-84 E to I-205 N into Washington to the first right for WA-14 E (exit 27 toward Camas) for 27 mi, or take I-5 N into Washington to the first right for WA-14 E (exit 1A) for 34 mi. From Vancouver, take WA-14 E 34 mi near milepost 35, and turn left (N) on Kueffler Road (opposite Beacon Rock) 1 mi to the sign for the equestrian TH on the

Phlox Point in the mist from the moss-lined path.

From the summit marker to nearby Table Mountain, Augspurger to Dog Mountain behind, then across the river to Nick Eaton Ridge up to Green Point Mountain and the closer ridge up to the Benson Plateau above Cascade Locks.

right. Follow this steep, somewhat rocky side road ¼ mi more to the end at the large parking lot.

ROUTE: Begin up the Hardy Ridge Trail (old gravel road) past the kiosk and gate, winding up a few turns almost 1¼ mi through the trees, with a couple of small creeks and decent signage, to a 3-way intersection, including the return trail for the clockwise loop (ignoring the "Lower Loop Tr" sign, which is for horses and lengthens the hike). Stay left (NW) for the wide W ridge trail on a fairly painless upward traverse 1¼ mi to the N. Climb right at a juncture up the narrow hiker's trail, a steeper and rockier stretch 1 mi NE with 14 switchbacks, to the signed saddle on Hardy Ridge ("2552 ft"). Views of Archer Mountain and the Columbia Gorge to the W become better after 10 switchbacks and the trees become sparse as you approach the saddle and high ridge. Mount Hood pops into view after the 11th switchback. Then you will have a picturesque scene with a narrow spiny ridge bump nearby toward the Gorge (S) and the rest of the long ridge the other way 1 mi N to Phlox Point. If you're worn out, by all means forget the mountaintop and head down the same way from the saddle; otherwise continue to the NE on Hardy Ridge Trail 3¾ mi to the TH for a 7¼-mile loop.

To reach Phlox Point, hike left (N) from the saddle up the ridge itself or just W without difficulty (steeper at first, then down slightly and up) on the slim, worn trail in and then mostly out of the trees, with wonderful panoramas on a clear day of big Cascade Volcanoes, the Gorge, and the nearby mountains of Washington and Oregon. Watch your step—Hardy Ridge becomes a bit steep and rocky—and pass a plethora of wildflowers (especially purple phlox), then a small rock pile almost 100 ft S of the summit cairn. Return down S to the saddle and turn left (NE) to continue the loop.

Follow the trail 1¼ mi down a pleasant grade on the E side of Hardy Ridge through the woods and 3 switchbacks, then a long widening straightaway S to a signed juncture at about 1800 ft. Bridge and Upper Hardy Trails take off left (N) toward the trails W of Hamilton Mountain or a side trip loop for a slightly longer trek (*see* the map on p. 175). Another ¾ mi S (see the top of Mount Hood SE) with one sweeping turn brings you to a 4-way convergence where the above side trip loop comes in from the left. Turn hard right to continue S for ½ mi down to the end of the main loop and proceed straight (SW) at the final intersection to finish the last mile-plus to the TH.

54 | THREE CORNER ROCK

ELEVATION: 3550 ft, with 1200 ft vertical gain

DISTANCE: 2¼ mi up, 4½ mi round-trip

DURATION: 1½ hours up, 2½–3 hours round-trip with a break

DIFFICULTY: Moderate. Wide, steep and steady, rockier, not lengthy

Birkenfeld to Table Mountain and Mount Hood past the relay tower from the old lookout.

TRIP REPORT: The route listed is the most enjoyable and is the shortest of the many ways to the top of this distinctive landmark off the beaten path from the standard Gorge hikes. It's also not mountain bike friendly like the much longer,

Three Corner Rock comes into view on the last bit of steep trail.

more difficult Three Corner Rock Trail SW of the summit all the way to Washougal River Road. No fee or restroom. Feel free to use this TH to tack on hike 55 as well.

TRAILHEAD: Near Rock Creek Pass. From Portland, take I-84 E to exit 44 (Cascade Locks), turn right up the circle to cross into Washington over Bridge of the Gods ($1 toll required), turn right on WA-14 E 1½ mi to milepost 43 (same locale from Vancouver on WA-14 E), and turn left on Rock Creek Drive toward Skamania Lodge, but take the second left on Foster Creek Road for ¾ mi into SW Ryan-Allen Road. Turn left on Red Bluff Road (FR-2000) 9¾ mi as the gravel road becomes steeper to Rock Creek Pass (at nearly 2200 ft) and a 4-way crossroads, where you stay left (SE) on FR-2090 for ¼ mi even steeper but okay for most in 2WD to the small pullout on the right for the PCT. An illegible yellow sign on its side ("CG 2090" with gunshot holes) is a clue at the pass. At 5½ mi up FR-2000 ("CG-2000"), cross a bridge over Rock Creek at a delightful waterfall area, then it's obvious to the pass staying left, left, right, left, right at any forks! It's less than 1½ hours of fairly easy driving from the Portland area. In winter, park below the steeper snow-covered part of the road and Rock Creek Pass 1 mi from the upper TH down N where FR-2000 crosses the PCT at a smaller pullout (1750 ft), and take the PCT from there, adding 3 mostly tranquil miles round-trip to the hike.

ROUTE: Follow the PCT S from the main (upper) parking area almost 1½ mi up the wider ridge section NE of Three Corner Rock as you pass through fir and hemlock to begin. Mount Adams dominates part of the view as you soon rise above 2 of 3 switchbacks to the Three Corner Rock Trail on the right. Take it almost ¾ mi SW to the summit by walking up to where the trail turns into an old road that you follow right again steeply and briefly to the flats and next junction at the saddle under the old lookout.

Scramble right (NW) a couple hundred yards more steeply up the path winding to the concrete steps and granite boulders. Making your way is easier than it appears from a distance, as you follow the posts to the top of the pile, where it becomes steeper as the path ends below the final few feet. Mount Hood and Mount Jefferson are S past the microwave tower. Mount St. Helens and Mount Rainier are N with Table Mountain, South Birkenfeld Mountain, and Birkenfeld Mountain to the SE, and you will also see Silver Star Mountain, the Indian Heaven Wilderness, Mount Adams, and of course the Gorge. Marinate in the moment and return by the same route for the best descent to your vehicle.

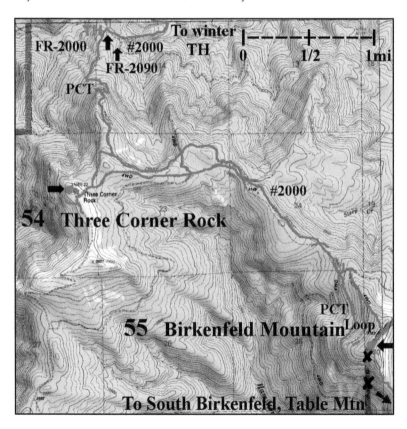

COVERS HIKES 54-55

> **"Forget not that the earth delights to feel your bare feet and the winds long to play with your hair."**
>
> **—KHALIL GIBRAN**

55 | BIRKENFELD MOUNTAIN

ELEVATION: 3763 ft, with vertical gains of 1663 ft and nearly 2000 ft, including Three Corner Rock

DISTANCE: 4½ mi up, 9 mi round-trip; 10½–11 mi round-trip with Three Corner Rock

DURATION: 2½ hours up, 4 hours round-trip; 5 hours round-trip with Three Corner Rock

DIFFICULTY: Strenuous. Steeper at times, wide into trail-finding, ups and downs, bonus summit

Mount Hood, Table Mountain, and nearby South Birkenfeld from Birkenfeld Mountain.

TRIP REPORT: A quiet route without crowds or much signage. A GPS device would help with so many logging roads, ATV, and bushwhacking trails in the area, or simply use the map here on p. 182. No fee or restroom.

TRAILHEAD: Near Rock Creek Pass. *See* hike 54 for directions.

ROUTE: *See* hike 54 for the detailed description, and follow the trail almost 1½ mi S until Three Corner Rock Trail breaks off to the right (W). Stay left (E) instead on PCT 2000 as the route becomes more level and even descends a bit through the trees just left (N) of the ridge itself. See Mount St. Helens, Mount Rainier, Mount Adams, the top of Goat Rocks, and finally the first looks at Birkenfeld and

Steep Creek Falls (52 feet high) from the drive to the trailhead near Rock Creek Pass.

Mount Hood. At 1¼ mi from the Three Corner Rock Trail, a confusing 5-way intersection and crossroads is alleviated by staying on the PCT just left of a large rock and small yellow sign (CG 1510) indicating the trail in the center of the ridge. Walk 1¼ mi to the second 4-way juncture, as you undulate up slightly and then go down past the saddle and first juncture to the next road crossing at almost 3200 ft. Turn left (NE) off of the PCT a couple hundred yards up to another little saddle and junction, disregarding a fork down left.

Turn right (S) at the little saddle onto another unmarked path for ¼ mi along an old ATV trail, following a smattering of flags. Bushwhack left off the trail at 3400 ft nearest a couple flags (one tied to a short post) and head up the NW ridge proper, as the last bit is fairly steep but easy to follow more than ½ mi once you locate the actual path; there is not much flora as you move through the thin pines to the very top, which is fairly nondescript over a large flatter area. The forest breaks up enough to make the hike pay off as you walk SW along the cliffy area and high ridge with narrow open meadows to the summit. There you will have decent views of Greenleaf Peak, the Columbia River, and the continuation of the ridge to South Birkenfeld and Table Mountain, with Mount Defiance and Mount Hood across the Gorge farther S, and other big Cascade Volcanoes including Mount Jefferson (on a clear day) never far from sight.

Return the same way back to the NNW for the best descent, or continue from the peak with a loop and more difficult bushwhack down the S ridge more than ½ mi to the PCT. Follow the rough and very steep path down through the woods to the wider PCT, where you turn right (NNW) for 1 mi on a traverse down to the crossroads with the main route and end of the summit loop. Return to the TH more than 3½ mi away on the PCT, or if you are hiking to Three Corner Rock, take the old road left from the ridge saddle and 5-way intersection in 1¼ mi for about 1½ mi directly W to the lookout and rock pile (turning right at the juncture more than ¼ mi from the 5-way intersection onto the rockier path that makes a beeline WNW toward the goal). Work up gradually by short pines through an old clear-cut with great shots of Birkenfeld Mountain, Mount Hood, and then Mount Adams. Pass narrower Three Corner Rock Trail on the right as the summit trail becomes much steeper briefly to the flats where you can see the remainder of the route. From the old lookout at the top of the boulder mound, follow the trails down left 2¼ mi N without trouble to the TH.

56 | SOUTH BIRKENFELD MOUNTAIN LOOP

ELEVATION: 3553 ft, with vertical gains of 3500 ft and 3800 ft, including Table Mountain

DISTANCE: 6¾ mi up, 13½ mi round-trip; 13 mi round-trip loop with Table Mountain

DURATION: 3–4 hours up, 5 hours round-trip directly and 6–7 hours round-trip loop with Table Mountain

DIFFICULTY: Very challenging. Long, steady up the PCT, steeper short trail to summit, very steep up or down Table Mountain, narrow and overgrown path N of Table Mountain

TRIP REPORT: Restroom present at Dick Thomas TH, where there is a day-use fee of $5 to park, payable at the Bonneville Hot Springs Resort and Spa desk. No fee or restroom at Aldrich Butte TH.

TRAILHEAD: Dick Thomas TH or nearby Aldrich Butte TH. *See* hike 49 or hike 50 for directions.

ROUTE: Follow the description for hike 49 or hike 50 less than 3 mi to the Heartbreak Ridge Trail intersection on the PCT. Continue on the easier trail left ½ mi to

South Birkenfeld to Birkenfeld Mountain along an open ridge section from Table Mountain.

Passing a large scree field from Table Mountain on the PCT to South Birkenfeld Mountain.

the next juncture, coming down from the N, the West Ridge Trail to Table Mountain. If you take the loop it will be noticeably easier in a clockwise fashion to come down the super-steeps of Heartbreak Ridge or the steeps of West Ridge Trail after summiting South Birkenfeld Mountain first, then onto Table Mountain and down, rather than ascending by these two routes.

For the direct route to South Birkenfeld Mountain, stay on the PCT on an ascending traverse NNW for a couple of stress-free miles in and out of the woods, then cross under a power line. Follow the main trail another mile (passing a logging road after ¼ mi) as you wind up to the saddle between Table Mountain and South Birkenfeld under the same power line. Turn left off the PCT (NW at almost 3200 ft) onto an ATV path coming from the logging road under the power line, and continue more steeply but pleasantly ½ mi straight up the Birkenfeld Ridge. The route narrows on the ridgeline to the nearby peak. Trees on the E side of the ridge limit the view somewhat, but not to the W where you can see Three Corner Rock, Silver Star Mountain, Mount St. Helens, Phlox Point, Hamilton Mountain, Mount Hood, and the Gorge!

Return the same way or continue N for a little summit loop ¼ mi down the ridge crest painlessly to the PCT, where you turn right (SE) for ¾ mi to the main saddle between Table Mountain and South Birkenfeld. For the loop with Table Mountain turn left (SE) down the ATV path past the logging road under the power line and climb a mile and only 200 ft or so up in elevation to the summit. The trail narrows E of a small bump, then becomes steeper and overgrown a few hundred yards to the clearing and juncture on top of the mesa. Pass West Ridge Trail (easier descent), then Heartbreak Ridge Trail (most difficult but with better views), en route to the mouthwatering vistas nearby on the southernmost point of Table Mountain above its colossal cliff band.

57 | ARCHER MOUNTAIN

ELEVATION: 2030 ft, with vertical gains of 1030 ft directly up NW ridge bushwhack and 1230 ft up more established trails; plus about 600 ft with ups and downs on loops for both routes to the overlook

DISTANCE: 2½ mi up NW ridge, 6 mi round-trip loop, including the spur path to an overlook and finishing on the main trail; 3 mi up more established trails, 7 mi round-trip, including a little loop above the overlook

DURATION: 1½–2 hours to the summit by both routes, 4–5 hours round-trip loops, including the overlook and Cynthia Falls

DIFFICULTY: Mix of moderate (easy to Cynthia Falls, wide, slight bushwhack to summit up more established trails, narrower, steeper at times) and strenuous (up NW ridge: very steep, drop-offs, trail-finding; high exposure near overlook: scrambling, quite steep and narrow but obvious from summit to overlook)

TRIP REPORT: The many trails and waterfalls that surround Archer Mountain (*see* the maps on pps. 191, 192) are less visited, unmaintained, and partly off-limits within the Columbia Falls Natural Preserve. This hike describes the best route to Cynthia Falls and the summit area. The W ridge of the horseshoe provides more difficult and steeper but interesting access to the mountain from the top of Smith-Cripe Road (between Cape Horn and Beacon Rock on WA-14), with a painstaking bushwhack to view Archer Falls near the N end of the cirque. More than 500 acres in the valley below Archer Falls are closed to the public. There is also a very hard

Top of Cynthia Falls.

scramble through the narrow canyon just W of Archer Mountain's W ridge up several quality hidden waterfalls on Gable Creek. There are few to no trails and private property in High Valley near that TH, making the route more confusing but worth exploring on drier days in the spring. An old path above and N of the hidden waterfall canyon is terribly rough if you are looking for a doable loop or entrance/exit option—not at all recommended at this time. The route to the summit over the W ridge not described here would take you down around 500 ft N of the horseshoe before rising 300 ft more S to the top. No fee or restroom.

TRAILHEAD: From Portland, take I-84 E to I-205 N into Washington to the first right for WA-14 E (exit 27 toward Camas) for 24 mi, or take I-5 N into Washington to the first right for WA-14 E (exit 1A) for 30 mi to Franz Road (past milepost 31½), turn left almost 1½ mi (see the menacing S face of Archer Mountain proper), then turn left on twisting Duncan Creek Road 1¾ mi. Park off the left side of the main paved road next to a 4WD dirt road under power lines. Or better yet, park around the nearby corner and bridge over Duncan Creek for more space as the pavement ends.

ROUTE: For the most straightforward ascent to this summit, hike the steep dirt and grass-covered road (there are no signs, but an old green gate is located a hundred feet up as a landmark) in the clearing under the power line almost 1¼ mi to the turnoff for Cynthia Falls. Turn left 300 ft a bit more easily, including along an overgrown stretch, to the base of the 50-plus-ft waterfall veiled in a minuscule slot canyon. In spring when there is a decent flow, you can barely see the black cables running through the creek bed. Return down to the main trail and hike up less than ¼ mi fairly steeply to view the falls again from the top for a better angle. Take the brief, unmarked, and unclear spur (being cautious) to the left just before the creek passes under the maintenance road as it levels off.

Walk left (S) at a fork above Cynthia Falls through the flats, past 2 side-by-side power line towers, to find the trail that widens after the initial bumps and stays right (W) of a small high point more than ½ mi, finally descending to a saddle on the ridge (2 mi from the TH). You may be able to hear Archer Falls or other falls below you, but there is no way to view the water from the trail on this side of the horseshoe.

The much steeper NW ridge bushwhack trail begins about a hundred feet from the little saddle, as you see a flag and narrow path to the left of the wider trail at a faint juncture. For this more difficult route, scramble up the super-steep and thin path nearest the ridgeline for ¼ mi, encountering a great viewpoint of the Gorge (left 30 ft to a tiny perch) and a small twin summit before the final ¼ mi on the disappearing path. The grade is improved as you watch for flags or plastic tied to branches along the wider, brush- and branch-covered ridge. Move to the right just before the very top and catch the stronger trail left at a juncture to the nearby tree-covered summit.

The hike and outlooks improve drastically if you continue ¼ mi SE and almost 400 ft down. The super-steep, narrow, and fun ridge path passes the easier return loop trail halfway, and follows mossy rock down a narrow spine. A bailout trail just to the right (W) avoids some of the drop-offs and meets near the end, where the rocky ridge widens a bit to the tip of the cliffy overlook and roost clearly visible on Google Earth or the equivalent! See Larch Mountain and Horsetail Falls in Oregon across the Columbia River, with Beacon Rock, Hamilton Mountain, and Hardy Ridge to the E. Finish much more easily by taking the return loop trail left (W) from the steep ridge, staying right (NW) at a couple of quick junctions, then left (W) at the next one steeply down to the switchback right (NNE) onto the main trail, and traverse up and down to the beginning of the NW ridge scramble juncture near the saddle 2 mi from the TH.

For the overlook directly and the summit approach on more pronounced paths, continue on the more leisurely trail from the NW ridge scramble route juncture near the saddle for more than ½ mi SSW to the next intersection. The trail narrows and becomes overgrown as you ascend and then lose 200 ft to a faint

Viewpoint from Archer Mountain to Larch Mountain across the river.

Archer Falls is blown, then freezes to the cliff walls in winter.

4-way intersection (at 1700 ft). Turn hard left (E) at the switchback to hike straight up much more steeply about ¼ mi directly to Archer Mountain, passing the much simpler loop trail to the overlook on the right at more than halfway. Descend to the overlook from the small summit plateau in the trees by either route, the ridgeline being direct, shorter, and more difficult with drop-offs. For the simple route from the juncture a couple hundred yards W of the peak, however, cruise left after attaining the summit, ¼ mi SE down to the same ridge by staying left (E) at a couple more faint junctions. Then finish to the right carefully like above from the steep ridge trail.

For a better look at Archer Falls (218 ft high), which dries up in summer and nearly freezes solid in winter, return to the main saddle under the power lines below the summit above Cynthia Falls, and hike the very steep road in the clearing a few hundred feet up to around 2000 ft in elevation. Look for a thin bushwhack path to the left (S), where you traverse a steep cliff line more than ¼ mi to a decent view of Archer Falls. If you miss that turn from the power line road there is another one at about 2200 ft, where you bushwhack over and down steeply to see the thin waterfall. The wind here more often than not blows the bottom half of the falls over the back of the canyon, as opposed to falling straight down, not unlike Mist Falls just W of Multnomah Falls in Oregon.

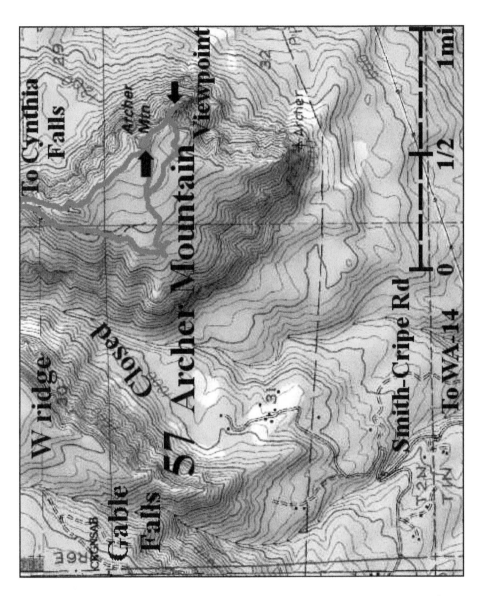

COVERS HIKE 57

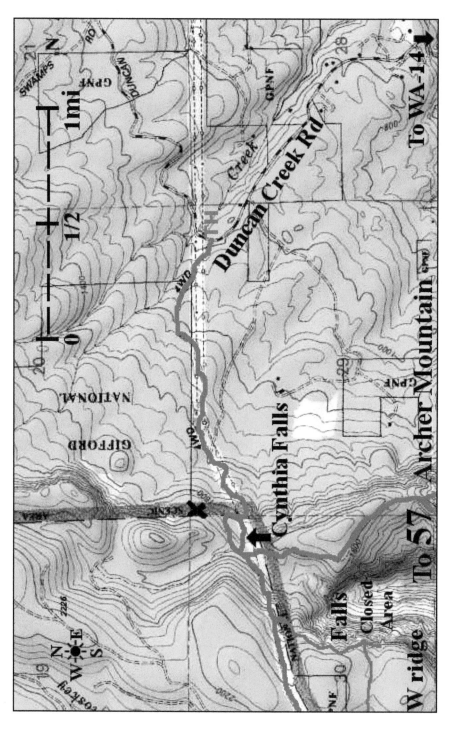

COVERS HIKE 57

58 | CAPE HORN LOOP

ELEVATION: 1280 ft, with around 1400 ft vertical gain for the loop

DISTANCE: 7½ mi round-trip loop

DURATION: 3–4 hours round-trip loop

DIFFICULTY: Mix of moderate (N of WA-14 no loop, popular, wide trail, some drop-offs) and strenuous (loop, some steeps, longer, cliffy, switchbacks)

TRIP REPORT: The lower portion of the loop is closed from about ¼ mi S of WA-14 to the bottom of Cape Horn Road from February 1 through July 15 to help protect nesting peregrine falcons in the area. Please respect the closed trail (yes, even though falcons, which can fly a flabbergasting 200 mph, have been known to thrive in urban areas and on busy bridges oblivious to human activity). This pretty much removes the possibility of hiking S of WA-14 during these months (except to Cape Horn Waterfall Overlook and Oak Viewpoint), but the Upper Trail is open year-round with fewer cliffs than the Lower Trail except at a few viewpoints without guardrails. Try a trip to the Nancy Russell Overlook from the main TH and back the same way (5 mi round-trip) during the closure. All of the trails here are more difficult when wet or icy, especially S of WA-14. Cape Horn Loop is family-friendly in that the routes are not severe but border cliff bands for much of the hike. Keep young ones close and dogs on a leash. There is no fee, and a vault toilet is present at the main TH. Simply follow the "trail" and "viewpoint" signs when in question; otherwise the loop is well marked.

Cape Horn Falls from the old trail.

TRAILHEAD: From Portland, take I-84 E to I-205 N into Washington to the first right for WA-14 (exit 27 toward Camas), or take I-5 N into Washington to the first exit (1A) for WA-14 E and drive several miles to milepost 26½ (1 mi beyond Cape

Horn Viewpoint), turn left on Salmon Falls Road for 150 ft, turn right on Canyon Creek Road, then right immediately into the parking lot (hint for those without vehicles: this is also a bus stop). Only 30 mi and 40 minutes driving from downtown Portland or Vancouver.

ROUTE: Begin the loop on the opposite side (W) of Salmon Falls Road, but then walk left at the nearby fork down to the tunnel under the highway to hike the loop clockwise on Cape Horn Trail 4418 (Lower Trail). The advantage to taking the loop in this direction is that you warm up by walking downhill along the somewhat less interesting road, and the rest of the day is filled with eye candy, as opposed to finishing the hike uphill in a more anticlimactic fashion. Continue from the highway bridge a couple hundred yards to Cape Horn Road. Stroll down right (SW) easily about a mile over the paved road past the ranches; see the highway, with Cape Horn Viewpoint to the right, across and far above a large meadow that you will eventually view from above.

A train moves under you looking west down the Columbia River from a lofty location.

Follow the signed trail to the right from the gated road near the bottom as you traverse SW over the bumpy path, climb up a couple switchbacks through the fern-lined steep forest, and then move up and down for a short time. The old path is rougher and steeper and used to lead hikers behind the bottom of Cape Horn Falls, but the newer trail omits this on a better grade over a bridge 1 mi from Cape Horn Road. This sexy little 60-ft (or so) segment is only part of the 600-ft-long seasonal cascading waterfall best seen from the Bridal Veil Falls area in Oregon as the final 250 ft drops directly into the Columbia River. From the scree field W of the falls, you can see another waterfall and more of the cascade up the rocks that is visible from the overlook above and Oregon in winter and spring. A few more waterfalls that you cannot see below you drop into the river during the same period.

Come down 4 switchbacks through moss-covered rock to a great overlook of Cigar Rock, a tall basalt column that sticks out from the rocky cliff band to the left (E) above the river. Nearby Phoca Rock juts up (25–50 ft, depending on the season) from the middle of the river and technically belongs to Oregon. Next a short bypass path to the right avoids the rest of the cliff band if you prefer. Continuing to the southernmost point of the trail (1½ mi from Cape Horn Road) along the cliff brings you to a pair of enchanting yet hazardous flat ledges without guardrails several hundred feet above the river. The longest tunnel in the Gorge lies directly below you, with an occasional train coming through. Use utmost caution observing the sights to the W: a slipup or fall would surely be dreadful.

Walk up a couple turns to meet the short bypass path when you're ready, and traverse left (W) past the old trail (right) and what used to be nearly 20 steep switchbacks through the talus field; the main trail has been relocated to protect the Larch Mountain salamander as a sensitive species by request of the Forest Service. The newer trail is almost twice as long, rising about a mile with a better grade for 7 steeper switchbacks and turns to meet the old trail again. This was reduced to a brief spur trail down switchbacks N to semiprivate Gorge vistas late in 2014, the fork to the left leading out to Oak Viewpoint with a large wooden barricade partially obscuring the river. Continue ½ mi NE much more easily to another outstanding newer tunnel under WA-14 with Cape Horn Waterfall Overlook along the way. The spur paths and handy rock work (completed by the Cape Horn Conservancy in June 2015) lead a few feet to one of the sweetest viewpoints on the loop! Hike N of WA-14 up several turns more than a mile without difficulty, through the woods and past a little collapsing shed with a decent roof to the Nancy Russell Overlook on a plateau at the top of Cape Horn. Phoca Viewpoint is another decent vista halfway up, as a horse trail veers away from the cliff line.

Friends of the Columbia Gorge founder Nancy Russell worked tirelessly to free up parcels of land to make the loop trail a reality with help from the Forest Service and volunteers from Washington Trails Association and Cape Horn Conservancy. The beautiful circular stone overlook provides some of the best views of the western Gorge and will be a sought-after destination for generations to come. See across the Columbia River to the rocky bluff out of the trees belonging to Angel's Rest, with the Larch Mountain shield volcano behind.

Walk more easily less than ¼ mi on the pathway from Nancy Russell Overlook to a dirt road, where you turn right (N) over the plateau for ¼ mi to the end at a big green gate. Turn left (W) on paved Strunk Road or the adjacent spur path for 150 ft and turn right (N) onto Cape Horn Trail again for 2 mi to the TH as you travel down, up, and down to finish. Stay right (S) of any forks (including near a power line below, where you can see Silver Star Mountain) to a couple more worthwhile vistas barely off the main trail, including Pioneer Point just below Fallen Tree Viewpoint (1¼ mi from the TH near another equestrian bypass trail). You begin to hear the highway sounds for the final dozen steeper switchbacks and turns on the Upper Trail through the open forest, before finishing across a small creek and arriving back at Salmon Falls Road.

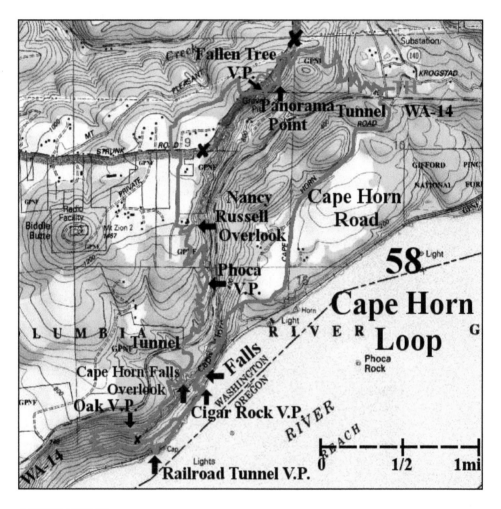

COVERS HIKE 58

ELEVATION: 4390 ft, with vertical gains of 1215 ft from the N for Silver Star Trail and Ed's Trail, 2015 ft from the S for Grouse Vista Trail

DISTANCE: 3 mi up, 6 mi round-trip or round-trip loop from Silver Star TH; 3¼ mi up, 6½ mi round-trip from Grouse Vista TH; 8 mi round-trip loop past Sturgeon Rock from Grouse Vista TH

DURATION: 1¼–2½ hours up, 3 hours round-trip directly from either TH, 4–5 hours round-trip loops from either TH

DIFFICULTY: Strenuous. Steady, wide, cliffy off of Ed's Trail, steeper up Grouse Vista Trail, scrambling, rockier

Autumn auburn is prevalent on the approach to Silver Star's double summit from Bluff Mountain Trail near Little Baldy.

TRIP REPORT: Silver Star Mountain complex within the Gifford Pinchot National Forest is the jewel of the western Columbia Gorge in Washington and not to be confused with the much higher Silver Star Mountain and ski area near Washington Pass in the North Cascades. The extinct volcano and massif can be seen from many localities in the Gorge, and by Portlanders who pay attention, especially in deep winter when you can see white caps on the mountaintops. Many trails and old roads surround Silver Star Mountain; this hike and hike 60 include only the shortest, most scenic routes to and around the high point. The drive to Silver Star (Ed's) TH has gotten worse in recent years, with many pot-holes, ruts, and odd trenches; the last 7 mi take almost an hour and require a powerful high-clearance or 4WD. (If you prefer, skip ahead to hike 60 for a much easier drive but slightly more difficult hike to this summit.) You can hike or snow-shoe the region year-round, but Ed's Trail will be nearly impossible from winter through early summer because of a steep pitch S of Ed's Arch that holds ice and snow. No fee or restroom.

TRAILHEAD: For Silver Star Trail and Ed's Trail, from Portland cross the bridge into Washington through Vancouver on I-5 N to exit 11 for WA-502 E, turn right (E) almost 6 mi, turn left in Battleground on WA-503 N 5½ mi (or take I-205 N to exit 30B, merge onto WA-500 E briefly into WA-503 N), turn right on NE Rock Creek Road for about 1½ mi as it becomes NE 152nd Avenue, and fork left on NE Lucia Falls Road 7 mi to Moulton Falls County Park. Continue ¼ mi farther, turn right on Sunset Falls Road (Co Rd-12) 7 mi to Sunset Campground, turn right on FR-41 through the campground past the outhouses on the left (hint), proceed across the river and up left to stay on the narrow, gravel, pothole-stricken, aban-doned road 3¼ mi, turn sharp right on FR-4109 (no sign, GPS device helpful) slowly down almost 1½ mi, and fork left (not right on FR-1100) up 2½ mi of the roughest stretch of road to the end in a turnaround with much parking.

ROUTE: Begin up the steeper Trail 180 behind the kiosk (with an old faded trail map of the area) or the wider old road to the left, as they both meet several times up the open ridge. After around ½ mi, Ed's Trail 180A breaks off to the left and follows the ridge and E side of the ridge crest, while the wider Silver Star Trail 180 meanders up steadily well below the W side of the ridgeline. Great views of Mount St. Helens, Mount Rainier, and Mount Hood already exist, and wildflowers will be popping up everywhere from late June through August, including bear grass, various lilies, paintbrush, sky pilots, asters, and phlox to name a few.

Walk up Ed's Trail for a more attention-grabbing variation or as a probable loop option with Silver Star Trail, as they meet again in 1½ mi just before (N of) the summit block. Keep youngsters close near Ed's Arch: the terrain becomes much steeper after (S of) the cool, rocky doorway you must walk through. If snow lingers or the rocks are wet, a semi-difficult to dangerous scramble may be neces-sary to stay near the trail, which might disappear on the traverse and may actually be 30–40 ft above you to the right, accessible normally from 2 steep, rocky switch-backs 100 ft after (S of) the arch. Perchance you'll notice a seasonal waterfall down the valley to the E before leaving the steep area after the arch. Contour SW briefly without any more difficulty to the main trail and turn left on Trail 180.

Hiking Silver Star Trail from the TH, you'll pass Chinook Trail 180B on the right ½ mi past the bottom of Ed's Trail. Sturgeon Rock will come into view

Ed's Arch in the clouds.

to the right (W) of Silver Star Mountain up the mostly treeless, wildflower-covered high ridge. A hundred yards after the juncture with Ed's Trail (E) near the uppermost part of the mountain, you arrive at a major intersection, where the slope holds snow until the last minute in early summer while the peak is bare and blooming. Turn left (E and SE) up the signed Spur Trail 180D less than ½ mi more steeply to the dual summit area, the N peak with the old lookout foundation being the highest. On a clear day Mount Jefferson and even Three Sisters can be seen far to the S, in addition to closer Goat Rocks Wilderness and Mount Adams. Even closer is Sturgeon Rock with Little Baldy and Bluff Mountain the other way (E) down the ridge.

If you want to explore farther and add 2–5 mi and 400–700 ft of vertical gain, you could take Bluff Mountain Trail 172 right (E) from the highest juncture N of Silver Star Mountain as far as you desire down an attractive, fairly narrow ridgeline and come back up the same way. One mile down is the connection with Stairway Trail 175 heading left (N), and in another mile or so the path begins to dip to the right of Little Baldy, where some folks bushwhack left with some difficulty to the top. Either way, the seldom seen views of Silver Star Mountain and its double summit from this angle don't get much better! Return to Silver Star Trail 180 and walk right (N) around 2½ mi on the wide old road down the left (W) side of the main ridge for the simplest route back to Silver Star TH.

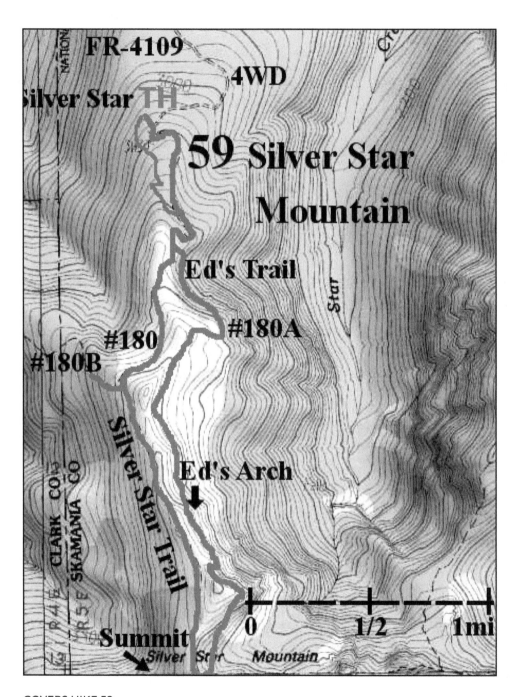

FR-4109

4WD

Silver Star TH

59 Silver Star Mountain

Ed's Trail

#180A

#180

#180B

Silver Star Trail

NATIONAL

CLARK CO.
SKAMANIA CO.

R 4 E
R 5 E

Ed's Arch

Summit

Silver Star Mountain

0   1/2   1mi

COVERS HIKE 59

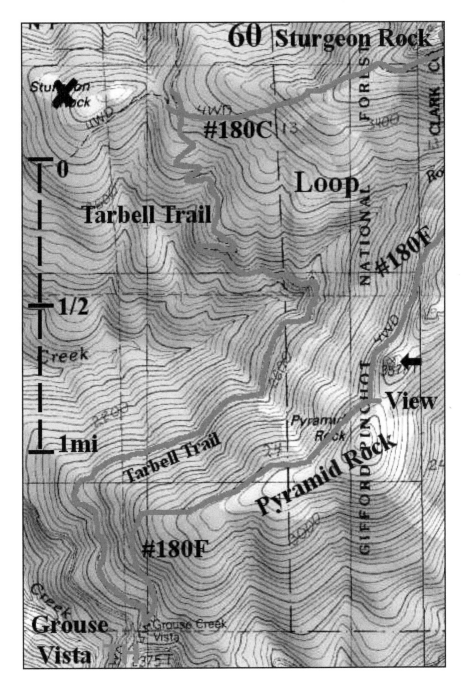

COVERS HIKES 59-60

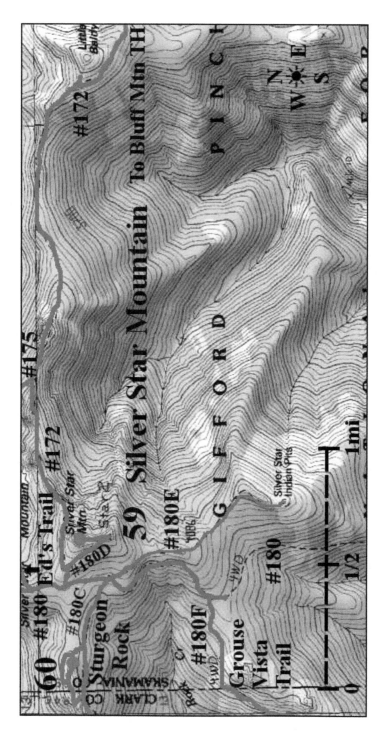

COVERS HIKES 59-60

60 STURGEON ROCK LOOP

ELEVATION: 4183 ft, with vertical gains of 1810 ft and about 2115 ft, including Silver Star Mountain

DISTANCE: 7 mi round-trip loop; 8 mi round-trip loop with Silver Star Mountain

DURATION: 4–5 hours round-trip counterclockwise loop with Silver Star Mountain

DIFFICULTY: Mix of strenuous (wide trails, rocky, some steeps, drop-offs) and expert-only (nearly vertical wall climbing option on Sturgeon Stairway, grassy ledges, rope not required, very brief)

TRIP REPORT: Discovery Pass required. No restroom.

TRAILHEAD: For Grouse Vista Trail or Tarbell Trail and the most direct routes to hike Silver Star Mountain or Sturgeon Rock, take I-84 E to I-205 N from Portland into Washington to exit 30 (Orchards), take the middle exit 30B for WA-500 E, exit immediately and turn right on NE Fourth Plain Road almost 1½ mi, turn left on NE Ward Road 3¼ mi into NE 182nd Avenue another 1 mi, turn right on NE 139th Street 2¼ mi, turn left on NE Rawson Road 5½ mi into L-1400 for 3 mi more, turn left on L-1000 (Larch Camp sign) 1¾ mi into dirt 2½ mi more, turn right on L-1200 for ¾ mi, and fork right on L-1200 for 4½ mi to the parking lot (only 1½ hours easy driving time from Portland, 1 hour or more from Vancouver). You can see Pyramid Rock and part of the route up to the left on the last of the drive to the saddle and parking.

ROUTE: The Tarbell Trail travels from the saddle and parking area behind the kiosk S and W to Larch Mountain (not to be confused with Oregon's Larch Mountain) in 2½ mi and with about 1000-ft elevation gain; it would make for a nice and easy side trip to tack on or save for a separate hike. Cross the road instead and begin steeply up the continuation of Tarbell Trail and beginning of Grouse Vista Trail 180F (unsigned, splits off) a hundred yards to the Tarbell Trail juncture and return loop option on the left.

Continue to the right (counterclockwise loop) up the steep, wide, rocky Trail 180F through the woods ¾ mi NNE before it begins to open up and level off a bit. Stay left of any junctions for almost 2 mi as you see the flat-topped Sturgeon Rock (and Sturgeon Fin) up to the left (NE) with Pyramid Rock towering above to the right (3577 ft). (Note that USGS maps are off for both of these.) One short spur path right (S) heads a couple hundred yards up to a small saddle just S of Pyramid Rock and provides a sudden full shot of Mount Hood. Hike through the thinning trees to the Sturgeon Rock Trail intersection, but continue to Silver Star Mountain's loftier summit for a side trip and the grander views first. For this, walk a couple hundred yards farther on Trail 180 and turn hard right on Spur Trail 180D less than ½ mi more steeply to the twin summit area.

After returning to the Sturgeon Rock intersection, heading far left (SE) would take you ¾ mi down and up to Silver Star Indian Pits on Trail 180E for a curious excursion. Turn right (W) instead down the wide Trail 180C almost ½ mi toward Sturgeon Rock, and leave the main trail onto the climber's path through the trees on the right (N). This leads to the clearing at the base of the vertical basalt columns on the E end of the summit block. The alternate route to the peak and Class 4 Sturgeon Stairway wall climb is to stay on the main trail past the summit to one of the steeper paths that veers to the right more easily up to the Sturgeon Fin, where you walk to the right (E) up the wider ridge section to the peak. It's a little airy on top, so be careful as you take in unique shots of Silver Star Mountain, Mount St. Helens, Mount Rainier, Mount Adams, and Mount Hood.

Columnar basalt that comprises Sturgeon Rock from the base before Sturgeon Stairway.

For the Sturgeon Stairway free-climb, work your way around to the N side of the summit block from the bottom of the sheer basalt columns by traversing carefully through a little annoying brush along a cliffy area without gaining much elevation for about a hundred yards or so. Then look 100 ft up the vertical rock for a landmark: a single small pine tree clinging near the top of the ridgeline about 100 ft W of the actual summit. Begin climbing up the mossy ledges toward the tree by staying a few feet left (E) of it, as the ledges are fairly far apart and the grass on them can be loose and thick to make matters even more troublesome. Check all of your holds, and once you reach the tree, brace yourself to visualize the final feet of the main crux. You may even partly climb the tree and jump to the highest rocks nearest the ridge, but use utmost caution whatever your last choices are on the mossy wall, as a fall would certainly be tragic. Once you attain the high ridge, the short walk to the left and the climax is much better, though a bit narrower again near the very top. Happily you won't

Sturgeon Rock to Silver Star Mountain and Mount Hood.

have to return down Sturgeon Stairway, which is steeper than any stairway I know of except maybe the one at my grandparents' house when I was growing up!

To descend, follow the widening ridge (Sturgeon Fin) down W more than a hundred yards and leave it to the left (S) on the most worn path briefly through the trees to the Sturgeon Rock Trail, where you turn right (W) less a mile a bit more easily to the next crossroads. Turn left (S) on Tarbell Trail for almost 3 mi on the counterclockwise loop back to Grouse Vista TH, as the solid path heads down steeper switchbacks the first mile, then contours leisurely by a stream and soon well under Pyramid Rock back to your vehicle. Another tremendous hike with much to be thankful for!

> "I went to the woods because I wished to live deliberately, to front only the essential facts of life and see if I could not learn what it had to teach, and not, when I came to die, discover that I had not lived."
>
> **—HENRY DAVID THOREAU**

ACKNOWLEDGMENTS

Thanks to ChartTiff Enhanced Geographic Data, Northwest Waterfall Survey, Anne Scalamonti, Mario Tomaino from Shephard Clinic, Oui Presse's Shawna and Margaret, and my parents for being the inspiration of my lifelong reverence for the great outdoors, while taking the family on fun and interesting camping trips every year and forcing us to walk for what seemed like an eternity as little kids through Cook Forest, a National Natural Landmark in northwest Pennsylvania.

INDEX

CPSIA information can be obtained at www.ICGtesting.com
Printed in the USA
BVOW11s0838030815

411245BV00002B/2/P